Journal of Consciousness Studies
controversies in science & the humanities

Vol. 12, No. 1, January 2005

2   About Authors

TARGET PAPER

3   A Plain Person's Free Will   *David Hodgson*

PEER COMMENTARY AND RESPONSE

20   Remarks on Evolution and Time-Scales   *Graham Cairns-Smith*

23   Hodgson's Black Box   *Thomas W. Clark*

33   Commentary on Hodgson's Paper   *Ravi Gomatam*

40   What Should We Retain from A Plain Person's Concept of Free Will?   *Gilberto Gomes*

43   Isolating Disparate Challenges to Hodgson's Account of Free Will   *Liberty Jaswal*

46   Free Agency and Laws of Nature   *Robert Kane*

53   Science Versus Realization of Value, Not Determinism Versus Choice   *Nicholas Maxwell*

59   Comments on Hodgson   *J.J.C. Smart*

65   The View from Within   *Sean A. Spence*

70   Commentary on Hodgson   *Henry Stapp*

76   Response to Commentators   *David Hodgson*

Published in the UK and USA by Imprint Academic, PO Box 200, Exeter EX5 5YX, UK
World Copyright © Imprint Academic, 2005. No part of any contribution may be reproduced in any form without permission, except for the quotation of brief passages in criticism and discussion. The opinions expressed in the articles and book reviews are not necessarily those of the editors or the publishers.

JCS is indexed and abstracted in: *Social Sciences Citation Index*®, *ISI Alerting Services* (includes *Research Alert*®), *Current Contents*®: *Social and Behavioral Sciences*, *Arts and Humanities Citation Index*®, *Current Contents*®: *Arts & Humanities Citation Index*®, *Social Scisearch*®, *PsycINFO*® and *The Philosopher's Index*.

ISSN 1355 8250   ISBN 1 84540 027 5

Cover photograph by Jacqueline Combes © 1994

ABOUT AUTHORS

David Hodgson is a Judge of Appeal in the Supreme Court of New South Wales. He has a keen interest in philosophical issues relating to consciousness and particularly free will. He is the author of the book *The Mind Matters* (1991) and has published numerous articles on these topics in this journal and elsewhere.

A. Graham Cairns-Smith was educated at Fettes College and Edinburgh University where he received a PhD in organic chemistry. His working life was spent at Glasgow University in teaching, pursuing ideas about the origin of life and the nature of consciousness, and researching protein chemistry, clay synthesis, iron photochemistry and crystal growth. He retired in 1997 and spends most of his time writing.

Thomas W. Clark is director of the Center for Naturalism and can be contacted at www.naturalism.org.

Ravi Gomatam is Director of the Bhaktivedanta Institute (www.bvinst.edu) and Adjunct Professor at the Birla Institute of Technology and Science, Pilani, India. He received his PhD in the philosophy of science from Mumbai University in 1998. His primary research interest is the foundations of quantum mechanics, with related interests in the philosophy of mind and of language.

Gilberto Gomes is a psychiatrist with an academic background in psychology and philosophy. He received his PhD from the University of Paris in 1998, with a dissertation on the theory of consciousness. He is associate professor at the Cognition and Language Laboratory of the Norte Fluminense State University (Rio de Janeiro State, Brazil).

Liberty Jaswal received his BA in philosophy from UC Berkeley, where he graduated with highest honours. He is currently pursing his PhD degree in philosophy at the University of California at San Diego. His interests are primarily in the philosophy of mind.

Robert Kane is University Distinguished Teaching Professor at the University of Texas at Austin, where he has been teaching since 1970. His many publications include *The Significance of Free Will* (1996).

Nicholas Maxwell is emeritus reader in Philosophy of Science at the University of London. He has written numerous books including *The Human World in the Physical Universe: Consciousness, Free Will and Evolution* (2002) and *Is Science Neurotic?* (2005).

J.J.C. Smart is an emeritus professor of Adelaide and Australian National Universities. At present he is an honorary research fellow of Monash University. He is an honorary fellow of Corpus Christi College, Oxford. His main interests have been in metaphysics (including philosophy of mind), philosophy of science, and also ethics.

Sean A. Spence is Reader in Adult Psychiatry at the University of Sheffield and Honorary Consultant Psychiatrist to Sheffield Care Trust NHS Trust. His principal research interest is the neuroimaging of volition in healthy subjects and those affected by neuropsychiatric disease. He has published in many peer-reviewed journals and textbooks.

Henry P. Stapp works with the Theoretical Physics Group at the Lawrence Berkeley Laboratory at the University of California. He has a particular interest in the quantum approach to consciousness and has published a number of papers in this field. His theory is set out in his book *Mind, Matter, and Quantum Mechanics* (1993, 2nd ed. 2004).

David Hodgson

A Plain Person's Free Will

In my experience, plain persons (here meaning persons who are neither philosophers or cognitive scientists) tend to accept something like a libertarian position on free will, namely that free will exists and is inconsistent with determinism. That position is widely debunked by philosophers and cognitive scientists. My view at present is that something like this plain person's position is not only defensible but likely to be closer to the truth than opposing views. To put this to the test, I have written a simple and straightforward outline of what I hope is a philosophically and scientifically respectable version of the plain person's position on free will, and have offered it for demolition by those who say such a view is untenable.

My account of free will is a robust one, explicitly inconsistent with determinism and intended to support equally robust views of personal responsibility for conduct. I see three broad areas of difficulty for this account.

1. The *randomness* problem: how can there be an intelligible and plausible alternative to determinism that is not mere randomness? Cf. Smart (1961).
2. The *moral luck* problem: we are products of genes and environment, so how can the way we are at any time and therefore the way we act be other than due to things outside our control, that is, be other than just a matter of luck? Cf. Strawson (1986; 1998; 2002).
3. The *supernaturalism* problem: science has given us a successful and comprehensive naturalistic account of how the world works, so is it not unreasonable to propose that human beings are somehow outside this account and outside the causal order apparently demonstrated by this account?

I address these difficulties in this article.

I: Nine Propositions

I will proceed by asserting and explaining nine propositions. I see the first five as basic requirements for any intelligible account of indeterministic free will; while the remainder are further explanations and elaborations of my own particular account of free will and responsibility. All these propositions have some

Correspondence:
David Hodgson, Supreme Court of NSW, Queens Square, Sydney, NSW 2000, Australia

relevance to each of the three problems I have identified; but propositions 3 to 5 are particularly relevant to the randomness problem, propositions 5 and 7 to 9 are particularly relevant to the moral luck problem, and propositions 5 and 6 are particularly relevant to the supernaturalism problem.

1. The <u>alternatives</u> requirement: there is a pre-choice state such that the way the world is and the laws of nature leave open at least two post-choice states

This is a minimum requirement for indeterministic free will. There must be a time before an exercise of free will by the doing of an action (or the making of some other choice or decision) when the action (or result of the choice or decision) is not uniquely pre-determined by the way the world then is and the laws of nature. There must be *alternatives* available: they may be the alternatives of two actions such as pushing button A and pushing button B; or of doing something and not doing it; or of shaping an action in one way and shaping it in another way. I say that the alternatives may also be the alternatives of making one judgment as to what to believe and making a different judgment, because I say that free will is exercised in making decisions or appraisals of this kind as well as in doing actions.

This requirement is intelligible, and is not implausible having regard to what quantum mechanics (QM) tells us about the world. Of course, there is the difficulty that, according to QM, any indeterminism is mere randomness, and I will return to this. There is also the difficulty that QM indeterminism may be at scales of mass, distance and time such that it cannot account for macroscopic alternatives like doing or not doing an act, or deciding a question one way or another.

This second difficulty does not affect intelligibility, and the degree to which it affects plausibility is a matter of controversy: I will not consider it in detail here. However, there are plausible suggestions as to how QM indeterminacy and indeterminism (perhaps together with chaos theory) could give rise to macroscopic alternatives: see Stapp (1998), Penrose (1994), Eccles (1994) and Jibu and Yasue (1995).

It is not part of this requirement that the alternatives be equally open, or that there be a sudden jump from a single pre-choice state to a single post-choice state. In some or even all cases, there could be a period of transition in which the likelihood of all but one possibility is progressively reduced to zero; and there may sometimes be extended processes of decision-making in which the likelihood of the various possibilities fluctuates significantly: see Hodgson (1999).

2. The <u>consciousness</u> requirement: the transition from the pre-choice state to a single post-choice state is a conscious process, involving the interdependent existence of a subject and contents of consciousness

This associates the exercise of free will with *consciousness*, and adopts a view of consciousness as involving the interdependent existence of a self or subject and contents of consciousness (cf. Honderich, 1987), with the subject taken as continuing as the same subject throughout the process of transition from the pre-choice state to the post-choice state. I will later argue that the subject in fact continues longer than this; but I do not contend, and my account does not require, that it be a 'substance' distinct from the brain processes that support it, much less an immortal soul. My account is rather a dual-aspect account of physical processes and conscious processes, with the subject being considered as the bearer or experiencer of the contents of consciousness.

The contents of consciousness may be generally described as *experiences*, but should not be considered as limited to passive contents: it is essential to an account of free will that subjects be considered as capable of being *active,* and this activity must presumably be reflected in the contents of consciousness. Again, this is intelligible and plausible: indeed, it is widely accepted that voluntary behaviour is active conscious behaviour.

However, some have argued that experiments by Benjamin Libet (Libet *et al.*, 1983) demonstrate that the real decisions are made pre-consciously, so that conscious free will can be no more than an illusion. In these experiments, participants were asked to press a button at any time they wished and to note the time of deciding to do so; and neural preparations for the action were recorded as occurring some tens of seconds before the time noted by the participants as the time of deciding to push the button. But it should be recognized that these experiments are applicable only to one kind of choice, namely that between doing and not doing an action; and even in relation to that kind of choice, show no more than that unconscious preparation is required before a person has immediately available the alternatives of consciously doing or not doing an action; and that is neither surprising nor inconsistent with conscious free will.

In specifying this requirement, I am not suggesting that all our motivation is conscious: plainly this is not the case. Nor am I suggesting that consciousness is other than a matter of degree: I am content to adopt the 'dimmer-switch' view of consciousness advocated by Susan Greenfield (1999).

I do not think I am succumbing to the myth of the homunculus in the Cartesian theatre (Dennett, 1991, Part II). Daniel Dennett convincingly refutes the idea that there is a central headquarters in the brain where consciousness occurs; but my proposition does suppose that there is. I accept that the physical processes that correlate with conscious mental processes occur over spatially extended regions of the brain, but this by no means precludes the existence or causal efficacy of conscious processes involving the interdependent existence of a subject and contents of consciousness. In so far as Dennett's rejection of the Cartesian theatre suggests the contrary, this depends on an assumption that causation must be local, as required by classical relativistic physics, an assumption which has been decisively undermined by QM (see Hodgson, 1996; 2002a).

3. The grasping requirement: in this conscious transition process, the subject grasps the availability of alternatives and knows how to select one of them

Again, this is a minimum requirement for free will. For example, if the choice between doing or refraining from doing an action is to be considered an exercise of free will, the subject must to some minimum extent grasp the possibility of either doing an action or not doing it, and must know how to do the action and also know how to refrain from doing it. This again is intelligible and plausible.

Once we have learnt to control our bodily movements, we are during consciousness generally aware that we can make various movements or not make them, and we know how to make them or not make them. This requirement accords with the Libet experiments mentioned above, namely that there must in general be non-conscious preparation before the choice process starts: it is plausible that there could not be conscious grasping of available alternatives unless this has been made possible by some preparation that must be largely unconscious.

In previous writings I have suggested that free will can also be exercised in the *shaping* of bodily movements, as distinct from their initiation. For example, when a pianist performs a well-learnt piece of music, consciousness comes too late to direct fingers to the right keys, but not too late to make choices in the shaping of musical passages. In such a case, I suggest, the pianist grasps the possibility of shaping the music in a particular way, and also is at least faintly aware of the possibility of shaping it in another way or else not consciously shaping it at all, and knows how to select either alternative; and thereby can respond consciously, and I would say freely, to sounds heard and emotions felt. This is part of the reason for the intense concentration that musicians report to be a requirement for their performances.

In those cases where we are faced with a choice or decision to be made between two or more explicitly-presented alternatives, whether they be alternative actions or alternative beliefs or appraisals, this requirement will plainly be satisfied.

4. The <u>reasons</u> requirement: in significant exercises of free will, the subject experiences reasons on which a selection can be based, reasons that are non-conclusive and thus can influence but not dictate the selection

I suggest that in significant choices we are consciously aware of experiences, thoughts (including thoughts in which we attend to *beliefs*), and/or feelings, that provide *reasons*, generally inconclusive and often conflicting, for one or more of the available alternatives. As mentioned earlier, I do not suggest that all our motivation is consciously experienced, much less that it is all consciously understood by us: plainly, much of our motivation is unconscious, and even the reasons of which we are conscious have a basis in extensive non-conscious processing. However, we do become consciously aware of feelings like pain or hunger, and of 'somatic markers' (to use a phrase from Damasio, 1996) associated with different alternatives, and also of beliefs and experiences relevant to our choices; and it seems that we are motivated by these feelings, beliefs and experiences.

It is plain that such feelings and other reasons are of diverse kinds, generally not measurable, and generally incommensurable. There is, for example, no common scale on which hunger for food can be measured against a feeling of obligation to carry out a promised task. That is one reason why it is a mistake to suggest that we act according to the preponderance of our desires: desires are not like forces in Newtonian physics that are commensurable and so can be combined to produce a resultant force. In general, the reasons experienced by a subject and relevant to a decision to be made by the subject do not dictate a conclusion. As I put it in Hodgson (1999), the reasons do not include a *clincher*; and as John Searle put it in Searle (2001), there is a *gap* between the reasons and the conclusion. The only clincher is the choice itself.

I cannot exclude the possibility that a choice between apparently incommensurable reasons is in fact wholly determined by unconscious processes, which are identical with physical processes that are in turn determined by measurable and commensurable physical properties and laws of nature; but the existence of that possibility does not justify disregard of this alternative account I am giving, or show that it is not intelligible and plausible.

5. The <u>selection</u> requirement: the subject makes an effective non-random selection between the available alternatives, based on these non-conclusive reasons, albeit not determined by rules or laws of nature

This is a vital proposition, one that is necessary to overcome the alleged dichotomy of determinism and randomness. It is a proposition which I've been advocating since 1991, following ideas of Nozick (1981) and Putnam (1983) (see for example Hodgson, 1991, Ch. 5, and particularly Hodgson, 1999), but which is still generally disregarded. If it is true, it is of enormous significance, *inter alia* in that it would show how different human beings are from computing machines as presently understood, no matter how powerful such machines may be or become. The contrary position, that what is not wholly determined by initial conditions plus laws or rules must be random, is widely assumed but rarely examined. It is considered with some care in Strawson (1986), but my opposing arguments remain unanswered.

It is convenient to consider first those exercises of free will involved in deciding between competing hypotheses or appraisals on the basis of inconclusive evidence. What is often overlooked is that, apart from rules of reasoning such as those of mathematics, logic and probability theory, there are no known rules (that is, strict rules as distinct from non-conclusive heuristics) governing good plausible reasoning. Of course, it is possible that plausible reasoning proceeds in accordance with evolution-selected computation-like procedures that we do not understand, and undoubtedly this is part of the story (I would say, that part concerning the determination of alternatives, reasons and tendencies); but there are powerful arguments for thinking that it is not the whole story, and that there is an element of *judgment* in plausible reasoning that is not accounted for by strict rules of any kind. These arguments include the following:

1. If choices were in fact determined by algorithms, such as evolution-selected computation-like procedures, which *as algorithms* need no help from conscious judgment and could indeed be hindered by conscious interference, there could be no plausible explanation of why evolution selected in favour

of brains that, at considerable expense in terms of complexity and energy-use, support conscious processes.

2. In particular, there could in that event be no plausible explanation (a) of why we have feelings like *pain* to motivate us, when it would be absurd (even if possible) to use pain or any other feelings to motivate a computer to proceed in accordance with its program; or (b) of why we are so constituted that our conscious awareness is automatically called into play when we are faced with a novel situation calling for decisive action.

3. Our rationality is well adapted to dealing with problems remote from the evolutionary tests that faced our evolutionary ancestors, and this makes it unlikely that it is no more than a matter of useful algorithmic processes selected through those tests: see Nagel (1986, p. 79).

4. If we cannot rely on our plausible reasoning as the conscious non-algorithmic process that we instinctively take it to be, then any confidence that we could have in it would have to depend on the circumstance that it comprises computation-like processes whose reliability is assured by the evolutionary tests they have passed; yet any belief in this circumstance and accordingly any justified confidence would itself depend on extensive plausible reasoning, giving rise to a vicious circle: cf. Plantinga (1993, Ch. 12), Nagel (1997, Ch. 7).

5. When we are conscious, our brain processes give rise to *qualia* (experiences or potential experiences) of various *types* and *chunk* them into unique *particular* global experiences of particular subjects: these are what I have called two tricks of consciousness, the qualia trick and the chunking trick (Hodgson 2002b). If a particular subject/experience combination produced by these tricks is to have a causal role in what happens, otherwise than through its *general* properties whose existence does not require this combination of tricks, then, because of the uniqueness and particularity of the subject/experience, this role cannot be one determined by generally applicable rules or laws of nature. Yet it seems clear that a particular gestalt or global experience, for example an experience of a unique and unprecedented work of art like Picasso's *Les Demoiselles d'Avignon* by the artist when he created it or an early appraiser of the work, does have a role in aesthetic judgments, a role that is part of rational appraisal yet which cannot be rule-governed because there can be no general rules that engage with a particular subject's particular global experience of a unique unprecedented object (see Hodgson, 2001, 2002b).[1]

This fifth argument applies to judgments as to what to believe as well as to aesthetic appraisals. In deciding what to believe on the basis of uncertain evidence, we seem to take into account our assessments of whole particular gestalt experiences; yet these experiences cannot, as unique and particular wholes, engage

---

[1] This argument, introduced in the first of these two articles and developed in the second of them, is I think an original and just possibly even an important argument. It is one of very few attempts to give a positive and non-mysterious account of why and how conscious processes can contribute to rational decision-making in a way not available to law-governed machines. I would refer readers to those articles, particularly the second of them, for a full exposition of this argument.

with general rules. For example, in deciding whether an experience is an accurate experience of some aspect of the world or is some kind of illusion or otherwise inaccurate, we take into account the particular global experience, and have regard to its clarity, immediacy, vividness, internal coherence, coherence with accepted beliefs, relevant similarities to experiences accepted as real, and so on. In such cases, I suggest, the outcome is not completely determined by the pre-choice state plus rules or laws of nature, but by a process that depends in part on a particular subject's non-algorithmic response to a whole particular experience. It is not reasonable to think that the outcome in such cases is either merely random or the result of some unique constraint that engages with the unique pre-choice state and no other: it is more plausible to think that it is the result of an indeterministic but non-random selection.

Roger Penrose (1994) has argued strongly for the view that human intelligence involves *understanding* of a kind that computers lack. My contention is that our access to and ability to use particular global experiences in a way that rules cannot determine is an important part of what is required for this understanding.

Similar arguments apply also to decisions about *what to do*, as well as about *what to believe*. What I suggest is that the ability of a conscious subject to take into account whole particular gestalt experiences, and to act upon judgments based on inconclusive reasons, has been selected by evolution just because it is more conducive to actions favourable to survival and reproduction than are purely algorithmic processes.

All this is confirmed by the powerful and ineradicable feeling we have that we are consciously making choices and making things happen by doing them. Suggestions, such as that by Crick (1994, p. 266), to the effect that we have this feeling just because we are not aware of the unconscious processes that are actually efficacious, provide no reason why any feeling of choosing or doing would be involved if this were the case. It would be as if I simply became aware of a thought and a movement of my body in accordance with that thought, without actually *making* a choice or *doing* an action. If this happened, surely I would not have any feeling of choosing or doing: rather, I would be puzzled by such an occurrence, in the same sort of way that the talking hemisphere of a split brain patient is puzzled by bodily movements initiated by the non-talking hemisphere.

This fifth proposition is probably the most crucial and difficult of my nine propositions. It is difficult, because we are so accustomed to looking for reductionist explanations, in particular explanations in terms of law-governed processes, and because in all fields apart from those involving questions about consciousness, reductionist explanations have been spectacularly successful. But while acceptance of this fifth proposition may go against the grain, I would argue that nothing is more familiar to us than our non-algorithmic plausible reasoning, which we can understand, to some extent at least, without making the reductionist assumption that it is no more than a small part of a wholly algorithmic iceberg that somehow gives rise to the misleading illusion that the processes of its conscious tip are rational but non-algorithmic.

Indeed, unless and until there is some other explanation of why we have conscious experiences and of what is their causal role, and also a satisfactory account of plausible reasoning in terms of algorithms, an account that altogether dispenses with judgments based on feelings and particular gestalts, I believe acceptance of this fifth proposition is more reasonable than its rejection.

Before leaving this proposition, I should note one significant attempt to give an evolutionary explanation of conscious experiences and their causal role, notwithstanding an assumption that they are constituted by and/or wholly depend upon computational algorithms carried out by our brains (see for example Dennett, 2003). This is to the effect that there have been evolutionary advantages for human beings and their close evolutionary ancestors in being able to monitor and communicate some of their own mental processes. Because these processes are too complex at the level of the computational algorithms (or any more basic level) to be grasped for monitoring or communication, evolutionary selection has developed brains able to produce simplified 'user-friendly' accounts of these processes, in terms of the existence of an integrated conscious subject or self that has conscious experiences, has goals and purposes, and chooses between available alternatives. These user-friendly accounts are not exactly false, on this approach, because at the level at which our brains can grasp their own processes for monitoring and communication, they give about the best available approximation to the truth; but they are not exactly true either, in that they tend to suggest that the brain's processes are other than the working out of computational algorithms, and to that extent they are false or at least misleading.

To anyone who strongly adheres to the view that our mental processes must be algorithmic, this approach may seem attractive. However, I think it has far too high a cost. A person's agonizing pain would be treated as an account of the person's complex of dispositions to act in certain ways, produced by the person's brain and thereby enabling the person to monitor and communicate relevant brain processes: it would have no other causal role, and in particular no efficacy in contributing to conduct by virtue of its subjective feel. Such a pain would be 'felt' no less by a Turing machine carrying out the same algorithms and thus producing the same account; whereas the brains of animals that do not monitor and/or communicate their mental processes would not produce such accounts, so that presumably those animals would not 'feel' pain even in this sense. I think pain has a reality, both as a feeling and as a motivator, that this approach denies; and I strongly disagree with the view (going back to Descartes) that no non-human animals feel any pain.

6. *Naturalism: there is nothing supernatural and no violation of physical law involved in such selections*

A standard complaint about libertarianism is that it introduces a supernatural element in order to account for 'contra-causal freedom', and that it involves violation of physical law. However, as mentioned earlier, QM and chaos theory make it possible for there to be macroscopic alternatives for selection, and QM shows that causation can operate non-locally so that spatially extended conscious processes could be globally efficacious.

Even when these points are accepted, it is still argued that, unless in every case one of the alternatives that are possible according to QM occurs at random within the probability parameters established by the laws of QM, then physical law would be violated, in the sense that the statistical predictions of QM would be falsified. However, it is reasonable to think that the felt strength of reasons has some relationship to QM probabilities, so that selections are likely to approximate to QM statistics; and having regard to the uniqueness and complexity of pre-choice states, a demonstrated violation of QM statistical predictions is unlikely in the extreme (see Hodgson, 1999).

More importantly, QM has not yet been applied to conscious systems, and it is an open question how its statistical predictions apply to such systems. The qualia trick and the chunking trick give rise to particular experiences of particular subjects; and if these whole particular experiences of particular subjects have an irreducible causal role in what happens, then, because of the uniqueness and particularity of the experiences and subjects, that causal role cannot be fully accounted for by any system of physical laws of general application, even those of QM. Indeed, my suggestion is that the capacity to respond to particular gestalts, to which rules cannot apply, has been selected by evolution just because this capacity is conducive to satisfactory choices and in that sense makes satisfactory choices more likely than they would be if choices occurred at random in accordance with QM statistics; so that, if it were possible to calculate them, the statistics of free choices would not be the same as if free will did not exist. This would not be a violation of physical law, but a limitation on the law's applicability.

This is not an appeal to the supernatural, but a recognition that the natural is not as narrow and limited as it is sometimes supposed to be; in particular, that it is not limited to the mechanistic development of systems in accordance with physical laws and randomness. I have previously argued (Hodgson, 2001) that laws of nature may be of different kinds, in particular that there may, in addition to laws that constrain outcomes (C-laws), be laws that empower systems to direct or select outcomes (E-laws) and laws that guide systems in such selections (G-laws). I there suggested that E-laws provide systems such as human beings with both the capacity to make selections and the reasons on the basis of which selections are made; and that G-laws include moral principles that affect such selections.

On that approach, exercise of a capacity to select is not contra-causal, but in accordance with a wider concept of causation. I do not suggest that the capacity to select appeared suddenly in human beings. Rather, I suggest it emerged very gradually in evolution along with the gradual emergence of consciousness. I believe that even primitive consciousness involves qualia and chunking, and may also involve the capacity to select. In primitive conscious systems, this might be exercised in such things as selecting in particular circumstances between getting food and avoiding predators. But I would not regard such capacity to select as amounting to free will unless and until combined with the self-conscious rationality of human beings.

7. Capacity to select: although differences between persons affect alternatives, reasons and tendencies, they do not otherwise affect capacity to select, which is the same for all persons

It follows from the above that a person exercising free will does so subject to considerable pre-choice limitations. The person has no alternatives apart from those made available by the pre-choice state and grasped by the person in the process of selection. The person has no reasons apart from those presented by the pre-choice state, generally based on non-conscious processes; and those same processes largely determine how the reasons feel and appeal to the person, and also give rise to tendencies to act in various ways. Another aspect of the pre-choice state, for which the person can have no responsibility, is that the person has the capacity to make a selection between the alternatives on the basis of the reasons. But I suggest that nothing in the pre-choice state pre-determines the result of exercise of that capacity.

The totality of 'the way a person is', prior to the selection being made, is inconclusive as between the available alternatives: it gives rise to reasons and tendencies to act in one or other of the ways that are open, but does not pre-determine the outcome. Thus the person's selection is influenced by the reasons and the tendencies, but not pre-determined by them. Indeed, it is reasonable to think that 'the way a person is', prior to the selection, does not affect the selection *otherwise* than through providing the alternatives, the reasons, the tendencies, and through the existence and exercise of the capacity to select. Different persons have different characters, and act differently because of these different characters. However, I am suggesting that this is because of the differences that pre-choice states make to alternatives, reasons and tendencies, not because of any differences in the persons' capacity to select. In relation to this capacity, each person is entirely the same, unaffected by differences in pre-choice states, whether due to genes, environment, prior selections, or all three; and in relation to its exercise, to the extent that each person can notionally be considered apart from differences affecting alternatives, reasons and tendencies, each person is entirely the same.

Thomas Clark (1999, p. 286) has suggested that this approach makes the choosing subject an abstract entity devoid of character and motives. The reverse is the truth. The subject is the unique totality of all its properties, and it is precisely because this unique totality together with particular experiences enters into the causal process that outcomes are not predetermined by constituent properties which it may share in varying degrees with other entities and with which general laws can engage.

We can't help having capacity to select, and nothing we can do *at the time of selection* can make us responsible for our particular characteristics that affect alternatives, reasons and tendencies; but our particular characteristics do not *otherwise* affect the way we exercise our capacity to select. We do this by choosing which alternative occurs, thus providing the clincher; and there is an element (by which I do *not* mean a distinct or severable element) of this process that is entirely up to us, unaffected by any differences between different persons. As asserted by the fifth proposition, this does not mean that the selection, or any part of it, is random or otherwise not rational.

8. *Moral principles: to greater or lesser extents, persons grasp moral requirements that should guide selections*

It could be argued that, even if persons have the capacity to make selections, that does not make it fair to treat them well or badly because of selections they make, because this would pre-suppose some objectively valid and binding standards of behaviour, and an ability in persons generally to know these standards. But I suggest it is intelligible and plausible to say that there are such standards and that persons can to greater and lesser extents grasp them. I mentioned earlier my proposal in Hodgson (2001) for a classification of laws of nature so as to include G-laws, which guide systems in making selections from alternatives open to them.

As suggested there, the grasping of G-laws could begin with the emergence in evolution of conscious systems, having some marginal capacity and reason to select and bring about one future state of itself, among those left open by the C-laws, in circumstances where there was fuzziness or conflict in the disposition or motivation of such a system as to what state should occur. For example, suppose that such a system felt, in a primitive way, something like what we would feel as motivation to minimize the pain of an injury, and also something like what we would feel as motivation to satisfy hunger; and that it felt it could follow one feeling or the other, but that following one would preclude following the other (getting the food would exacerbate the pain). The system, having these conflicting feelings, and feeling itself motivated by them towards differing future states of itself, both of which were open to selection by it, could I suggest also feel something like a requirement to resolve them 'rightly', and to bring about one state of itself (that is, *to act*) in accordance with that resolution.

This suggests the most basic G-law, which would to some degree guide and be felt by even such a primitive conscious system, a law which I call 'act rightly':

Act so as 'rightly' to resolve fuzziness or conflicts of motivation.

I use 'rightly' at this stage without any moral implications, so that the law here simply means, do whichever of the conflicting possibilities is apt or fitting or appropriate or 'to be done'. I say this law would be *felt*, because its guidance would, to some extent at least, take effect through its influence being felt and acted upon by the system itself. In more complex conscious systems, the basic G-law could come to separate out into two distinct aspects or sub-laws, which I call 'decide rightly' and 'carry out':

Decide what act would rightly resolve fuzziness or conflicts of motivation;

and

> *Carry out that decision.*

In such systems, selections could be assisted by further G-laws and/or by principles associated with them. In particular, these systems could feel and apply a G-law, which I call 'find out':

> *Optimise the reasons (including information and feelings) on the basis of which to act.*

In moderately primitive conscious systems, this could be felt as requiring attention to relevant information-and-feelings, as delivered by the senses and emotions. In more elaborate conscious systems, it could be felt as requiring such things as exploration of relevant information-and-feelings, verification by checking, looking for coherence and consistency, attending to analogies, and seeking an understanding of issues facing the system.

In conscious systems without the self-conscious rationality of human beings, the application of G-laws would not be a matter of morality, although analogies with human moral issues could be drawn. For example, some conflicts of motivation could be analogous to human moral conflicts, such as a conflict between an animal's motivation to minimize its own pain and its motivation to protect its offspring; and some actions by animals may display 'virtues' of courage and determination in carrying out decisions as to what act would be 'right'. However, in systems with self-conscious rationality, G-laws could have central moral significance. The basic G-law 'act rightly', as it applies to these systems, could be the fundamental moral prescription. Moral laws such as 'do no harm', 'be fair', 'be honest', 'fulfil commitments' and 'do good' could be further G-laws felt by these systems. Plainly, these further moral laws can conflict with each other, and they can also conflict with a system's basic motivating feelings. In such cases, the basic G-law would require the conscious systems to resolve conflicts rightly, having regard to all relevant G-laws.

Another G-law that a rational self-conscious system could feel is the following moral law, which I call 'improve oneself':

> *Enhance one's own ability to find out, decide rightly, carry out, and do good.*

This law would require the cultivation of virtues associated with the seeking of truth, particularly in so far as the truth was relevant to one's own actions; and of virtues associated with readiness, willingness and ability to put decisions rightly made into effect, and also to enlarge one's opportunities to do good.

Thus, in systems with self-conscious rationality, the G-laws, which I conjecture are laws of nature that are to some degree felt by all conscious systems, could come to be felt as being or including a system of guiding moral laws, which are truly existing features of the universe, ascertainable and to be respected by us whether we like it or not. Although such a view is very unfashionable today in some circles, some such view is required if, for example, an opinion that it is wrong to torture children for amusement is to be considered a matter of *truth* rather than merely something we have been programmed to believe by evolution and education. There is no greater problem with saying that the truth of such moral rules can be supported by plausible reasoning than, for example, with saying that the truth of factual inductive conclusions can be supported by plausible reasoning. There could be disagreement as to what it is that G-laws require in particular circumstances, and as to what, among rules which people claim to be moral laws, are G-laws or rightly derived from G-laws and what are merely fallible human inventions; although I don't think there would be much room for disagreement about the G-laws I have identified, most or all of which are I suggest to some extent grasped by all persons of reasonable mental capacity and sanity.

9. Ultimate responsibility: accordingly, there is some ultimate responsibility for selections, and thereby for subsequent pre-choice states

On this account, then, persons generally have alternatives open to them in their conscious behaviour, and feel reasons for selecting among these alternatives, including reasons associated with their grasp of moral principles such as those discussed above. 'The way a person is' provides alternatives, reasons (including the grasp of moral principles), tendencies and capacity to select, but does not otherwise influence the selection. Thus I suggest that, in making selections, persons do have some *ultimate* responsibility, with degrees of responsibility affected by how hard it is, by reason of the pre-choice state, to make the right selection. I do accept that these degrees of responsibility may vary widely, so that, for example, environmental disadvantages such as abuse in childhood may enormously reduce responsibility and blameworthiness for later conduct.

I earlier suggested that subjects continue throughout processes of selection; and now I suggest that it is reasonable to see this continuance as indicative of a more extensive continuance, throughout longer periods of deliberation on problems, and indeed throughout a whole integrated life-history that can be regarded as a progressive and continuous addressing of life's challenges (Hodgson, 1999; 2001). A conscious system comes into existence at or prior to the birth of a human being and continues as a system with the same subject, at least until this continuance is interrupted or terminated by significant brain injury or mental illness, or death. Thus there can be justice in treating a person differently according to what that person has done in the past, not just because the person has some ultimate responsibility for what was done, but also because the person is in a substantial sense *the same* person both at the time of the action and at the time of the subsequent treatment.

Furthermore, since prior selections, for which a subject has some ultimate responsibility, can in turn affect later pre-choice states of the same subject, the subject has some ultimate responsibility also for those later pre-choice states and thereby additional responsibility for what is done at later times.

II: Three Questions

I will conclude this essay by considering three questions about the account of free will given in my nine propositions.

1. Does this account involve agent causation?

One prominent version of indeterministic free will embraces a distinction between what is called event causation and what is called agent causation. The former is causation by events or happenings in the world, which is the causation dealt with by the physical sciences; and the latter is causation by agents rather than events, which is the causation supposed to be involved in exercises of free will.

In one sense my account of free will involves causation by agents, in that I suggest that a subject or agent persists throughout a process of selection (indeed, generally throughout a life) and actually makes the selection on the basis of inconclusive reasons: as I have put it, in selection the agent provides the clincher that finally determines which alternative out of those open actually occurs. However, I do not draw a sharp distinction between causation by events and causation by agents.

For one thing, I do not say that causal processes not involving subjects or agents must be analysed in terms of events: analysis in terms of things or processes or states of affairs may be equally or more appropriate for certain purposes. I do not think it is helpful to debate whether the world *really* is made up of things or events or processes or states of affairs, or whether causation is *really* causation by things or events or processes or states of affairs. There are things and events and processes and states of affairs, and consideration of questions of causation may involve any one or more of these categories: none I suggest needs to be considered as being more basic than the others.

More importantly, I suggest that events do have an important role in exercises of free will. Events have a role at least in limiting available alternatives and in providing reasons and tendencies; and the selection itself can be regarded as an event. The causation of the selection might be considered as being partly by other events and partly by the activity of the conscious subject or agent exercising its capacity to select; but even that analysis could be misleading, in that I regard the selection process as a global process, not divisible into distinct parts. So rather than distinguishing causation by events and causation by agents, I prefer to distinguish *physical causation*, which is that aspect of causation capable of being fully understood in terms of the operation of laws of nature and randomness, and *volitional causation*, in which the conscious activity of a subject or agent makes a contribution that can't be fully understood in that way.[2]

On my account, then, the nature and degree of responsibility of an agent for the agent's conduct can be a matter for rational consideration; whereas on the

---

[2] My view may be closer to the standard agent-causation view than is that of Robert Kane (1996), and it may be that Kane does not accept my fifth proposition. I think the criticism of Kane by Dennett (2003, Ch. 4) in fact, rightly or wrongly, assumes that Kane does not accept this proposition.

standard 'agent causation' account, causation by agents seems to be mysterious, absolute and incapable of further explanation.

2. *Does this account deal with the randomness problem and the moral luck problem?*

I mentioned earlier the *randomness* problem, the problem of making intelligible an alternative to determinism that is not mere randomness, and the problem of giving an intelligible answer to the *moral luck* argument.

The substantial answer to the randomness problem is that given in the discussion of the fifth proposition: but to see if the problem is really answered, it is useful to look at two elaborations of the problem given by Peter van Inwagen (2002).

In the first, van Inwagen supposes that God repeats many times a person's pre-choice state, and that (as required by libertarianism) on some occasions the decision goes one way and on others it goes another way. He supposes that, as the repetitions continue, the statistics of the choices appear consistent with a certain probability for each decision. He suggests that free choice is thus indistinguishable from random occurrences within probability parameters.

But as stated above, on my account of free will the statistics of many choices would not necessarily be the same as the statistics suggested by the laws of QM as applied to the pre-choice state that is repeated in this way, because the QM statistics would not take into account the subject's particular gestalt experiences that are part of the pre-choice state. The subject's selected response to the particular experiences is, for evolutionary reasons, more likely to be conducive to survival and reproduction than random occurrences within QM probability parameters.

In the second, van Inwagen supposes a choice between upholding public morality and betraying a friend on the one hand, and keeping silent on the other hand, in which the pre-choice state gives only just over 0.5 probability of keeping silent. Van Inwagen asks whether a person, knowing this probability, could in good conscience promise the friend to keep silent, when there is over 0.4 probability that the promise will not be kept.

On my account of free will, the probability given by the pre-choice state is at best a QM probability that does not take into account all relevant factors, including the particular gestalts of the pre-choice state; and in any event, the person will be able to freely choose what to do when the time comes. Furthermore, plainly the making of the promise will affect the pre-choice state, presumably making it more likely that what is promised will be done. But finally, if a person concluded that, even if the promise were made, he or she could not be confident of keeping the promise, that would be a strong reason for saying that the promise could not in good conscience be made. In this respect, libertarianism is in no worse case than competing views.

Turning to the moral luck argument, Galen Strawson elaborates on this argument in Strawson (2002), building on two premises:

1. We act as we do because of the way we are.
2. We cannot be responsible (in the sense of *ultimately* responsible, the buck stopping with us) for the way we act unless we are responsible for the way we are.

He goes on to argue that we cannot be responsible for the way we are when we first make decisions in life, so we cannot be responsible for actions based on those decisions, or for how those decisions and actions affect the way we are later on; and so on. Thus, we can never become responsible for the way we are later in life, or responsible for the way we act later in life.

He suggests that there can be no argument with his first premiss and, relying partly on the first premiss, argues powerfully in support of the second premiss.

What I say to this is that it is necessary to bring out an ambiguity in the word 'because' in the first premiss. It could mean that the way we are plus our circumstances plus the laws of nature pre-determine the way we act in those circumstances; and if it means that and is true, then it is hard to argue with the second premiss. However, on my account of free will, 'because' in the first premiss means that the way we are plus our circumstances plus laws of nature provide alternatives, inconclusive reasons and tendencies, and also the capacity to select between the alternatives on the basis of the reasons; and what we do is what we select in exercise of that capacity, the selection not being influenced by any differentiating features of the way we are *otherwise* than through the alternatives, reasons and tendencies. If the first premiss is true on that interpretation of 'because', the second premiss is untrue; and the Strawson argument collapses.[3]

3. Is this account believable?

As noted earlier, there is a question mark over the first proposition in terms of the availability of macroscopic alternatives. The fifth proposition is difficult, but in my contention difficult mainly because of ingrained habits of thought; and for reasons I have given I believe it is reasonable to accept it at the present time. The eighth proposition is highly unfashionable; but I think that at least some moral opinions are matters of fact and truth rather than mere evolutionary artefacts, and thus that it is reasonable to accept my eighth proposition.

---

[3] In his recent impressive exposition of a compatibilist view of free will and responsibility, Dennett (2003) does not refer to Galen Strawson or the moral luck argument. He does set out a related argument, along the following lines: what we do is wholly determined by events in the distant past and laws of nature; those events and laws are not 'up to us'; therefore what we do is not up to us. He claims (pp. 126–36) that this argument commits the same fallacy as an argument that there couldn't be mammals: if there have been any mammals, there have been only a finite number of them; every mammal has a mammal for a mother; therefore if there have been any mammals, there have been an infinite number of them. However, the fallacy in this argument is that there is an indeterminate boundary between mammal-like reptiles and reptile-like mammals; and while it may be said that there is a similar indeterminate boundary between actions in our early lives that are in no sense 'up to us' and actions in our later lives that are in some sense up to us, this does not deal with Strawson's premisses 1 and 2 and thus does not answer Strawson's moral luck argument. I suggest that something like my propositions 5 and 7 to 9 is required to answer that argument.

Reductionist science has had enormous success in accounting for many aspects of the universe, but very little success in explaining consciousness and its role in the way events unfold in the world. I think it is reasonable to believe that consciousness does have an important and irreducible causal role, and I suggest that something like this version of free will is required to account for this role.

So all in all, I say my account is believable, indeed at present more so than any alternative.

References

Clark, T. (1999), 'Fear of mechanism', in Libet *et al.* (1999).
Crick, F. (1994), *The Astonishing Hypothesis* (London: Simon & Schuster).
Damasio, A. (1996), *Descartes' Error* (London: Macmillan).
Dennett, D. (1991), *Consciousness Explained* (New York: Allen Lane).
Dennett, D. (2003), *Freedom Evolves* (London: Allen Lane).
Eccles, John (1994), *How the Self Controls its Brain* (Berlin: Springer).
Greenfield, Susan (1999), 'How might the brain generate consciousness?', in *From Brains to Consciousness*, ed. S. Rose (London: Penguin).
Hodgson, D. (1991), *The Mind Matters* (Oxford: Oxford University Press).
Hodgson, D. (1996), 'Nonlocality, local indeterminism, and consciousness', *Ratio*, **9**, pp. 1–22.
Hodgson, D. (1999), 'Hume's mistake', in Libet *et al.* (1999).
Hodgson, D. (2001), 'Constraint, empowerment, and guidance: a conjectural classification of laws of nature', *Philosophy*, **76**, pp. 341–70.
Hodgson, D. (2002a), 'Quantum physics, consciousness, and free will', in Kane (2002).
Hodgson, D. (2002b), 'Three tricks of consciousness', *Journal of Consciousness Studies*, **9**, pp. 65–88.
Honderich, T. (1987), 'Mind, brain and self-conscious mind', in *Mindwaves*, ed. C. Blakemore and S. Greenfield (Oxford: Blackwell).
Jibu, M. and Yasue, K. (1995), *Quantum Brain Dynamics and Consciousness: An Introduction* (Amsterdam: Benjamin).
Kane, R. (1996), *The Significance of Free Will* (New York: Oxford University Press).
Kane, R. (ed. 2002), *Oxford Handbook of Free Will* (New York: Oxford University Press).
Libet, B., Gleason, C., Wright, W. and Pearl, D. (1983), 'Time of conscious intention to act in relation to onset of cerebral activities (readiness potential): the unconscious initiation of a freely voluntary act', *Brain*, **106**, pp. 623–42.
Libet, B., Freeman, A. and Sutherland, K. (ed. 1999), *The Volitional Brain* (Exeter: Imprint Academic).
Nagel, T. (1986), *The View From Nowhere* (New York: Oxford University Press).
Nagel, T. (1997), *The Last Word* (New York: Oxford University Press).
Nozick, R. (1981), *Philosophical Explanations* (New York: Oxford University Press).
Penrose, Roger (1994), *Shadows of the Mind* (Oxford: Oxford University Press).
Plantinga, A. (1993), *Warrant and Proper Function* (New York: Oxford University Press).
Putnam, Hilary (1983), *Reason, Truth, and History* (Cambridge: Cambridge University Press).
Searle, John R. (2001), *Rationality in Action* (Cambridge MA: MIT Press).
Smart, J.J.C. (1961), 'Free-will, praise and blame', *Mind*, **70**, pp. 483–94.
Stapp, Henry (1998), 'Pragmatic approach to consciousness', in *Brain and Values*, ed. K.H. Pribram (Hillsdale, NJ: Erlbaum).
Strawson, G. (1986), *Freedom and Belief* (Oxford: Oxford University Press).
Strawson, G. (1998), 'Luck swallows everything', *Times Literary Supplement*, 26 June, pp. 8–10.
Strawson, G. (2002), 'The bounds of freedom', in Kane (2002).
Van Inwagen, P. (2002), 'Free will remains a mystery', in Kane (2002).

Commentaries On David Hodgson
'A Plain Person's Free Will'

REMARKS ON EVOLUTION AND TIME-SCALES

Graham Cairns-Smith

David Hodgson's highly stimulating paper argues that contrary to much expert opinion it is probable that we do indeed have 'free will', and more or less in the everyday sense of that term. I am inclined to agree, although I suspect that we will have to settle for a somewhat weaker version of the Plain Person's ideal.

Anyway the plain person is not always right. The plain person in me is inclined to talk of the sun rising in the morning: I have the sensation of a rising sun, not of a rotating Earth. So perhaps my feeling of free will is similarly an illusion. Perhaps we are not free to think and act as we will, but have only an ineffective feeling of such a freedom. It is certainly plausible and Crick (1994) in particular has put a neat argument for this position. But it is by no means certain, for reasons which David Hodgson discusses and to which I would add a few words.

In the 1870s William James realised that if feelings and sensations evolved (through natural selection in the way that Darwin had recently suggested for evolution generally) then feelings and sensations must be real and effective. If they evolved they must have physical effects, because features of organisms that had no physical effects could never be selected, could never take part in the Darwinian process. Now that the key idea of natural selection is part of the bedrock of science it has become perverse to deny that such well adapted feelings as hunger, lust, pain, and so on, evolved: and natural to accept James's deduction that our consciousness is not only caused by brain action, but that it also has effects, presumably in the first place on physical events in the brain (Glynn, 1993; Cairns-Smith, 1996). Surely, then, our feelings and sensations are part of the machinery of our behaviour, even if interwoven with unconscious neuroelectrochemical activity which is no doubt in control of most of our detailed actions.

But what of thinking and those critical points of decision within it? The plain person in me says that in making a difficult decision I may try to be informed, careful, reasonable…, but at the last point I go by what feels right. It seems that this is the way that 'Searle's gap' (referred to in Hodgson's Proposition 4) is filled. I notice that other plain persons seem to suppose likewise, in that they often use the word *feel* in place of *think* (as in 'I can't help feeling…', or 'the feeling of the committee', and so on). And it seems that the more difficult a decision is, the more conscious it is, the more it has to do with feelings. This might be taken as an indication that if there is part of our mind that has a special freedom then it is the conscious part, whether in an agony of indecision or in a sense of power to choose — or with intellectual feelings of 'rightness'; or with moral feelings which Hodgson refers to (Proposition 8). I don't think such feelings are accidental side effects. The agonies or the ecstasies here, as elsewhere in our consciousness, are too appropriate, too well adapted to be other than products of evolution and hence, in line with James's argument, to be effective, as they seem to be.

Brain research in the twentieth century made it more likely that conscious feelings have a causal role — important enough to explain the associated neural machinery being discovered. At the same time the scope for conscious control has reduced. I refer particularly to the remarkable experimental observations made by Grey Walter (described in Dennett, 1991) and more extensive research by Libet and others which Hodgson refers to. Conscious decisions come more slowly than they seem to, so much so that they cannot exert moment by moment control in, for example, rapidly moving sports or playing the piano. It is clear that any conscious action operates on a relatively slow time-scale, so that conscious 'free will', if it exists, takes at best about half a second to come into play (usually longer).

Such delays have been taken as a straight disproof of the efficacy of consciousness, but they can just as well be seen in terms of a contraction in the perceived scope of conscious control. The reflex that withdraws the finger from the touched hot-plate is far faster than the pain that comes too late to save us. But that is not to say that the pain is pointless, only that it is part of a longer term agenda, of learning. And then indeed we have to admit that it is only slower moving features of such activities as fast sports or piano playing that are open to there-and-then conscious control, say in *shaping* a musical phrase as Hodgson suggests.

There has always been a good practical reason for assuming free will, whether in the last analysis it exists or not. When Shakespeare's Julius Caesar (1600) seeks to cut out further discussion by saying 'The cause is in my will' he is, whatever else, being practical. Even if he had had a mind to, he would have been unable to explain *all* the reasons for his decision. The prior web of causes and effects that might be said to account for the state of a brain at a particular moment, and determine the next moment, is not only complicated and dense beyond hope of discovery, it is incomplete. If molecular chaos didn't foil us here, quantum mechanics would.

This takes us to 'the randomness problem' as Hodgson calls it. Is the freedom in 'free will' just randomness — mere chance?

Here I have a sense of *déjà vu*, because those who would wish to dismiss the idea of evolution though natural selection, often say something to the effect that they can't believe that all the forms of life on Earth arose 'just by chance'. Indeed chance is an important component in evolution, but it is not *mere* chance. It is chance-plus-selection that can climb mountains of improbability and which has given rise to the amazing contrivances of living things (Dawkins, 1986; 1996). Perhaps there is an analogy (no more than that) with the development of an individual mind in that this too comes from a concatenation of events within a framework that exerts 'selection pressures' for some outcomes rather than others — among these pressures are the mores of society. Thus little random acts of freedom that lead to personal satisfaction are reinforced, while others that do not are suppressed. What happens as a result is not 'mere chance' here, any more than with evolution, but something a good bit more interesting. The outcome is a unique truly unfathomable personality: an object that includes a propensity to think and feel, and feels that within the limits of circumstance it can do what it wants.

The plain person in me is almost satisfied with that, but awaits further developments. The trouble is that even if feelings are part of the machinery of our behaviour this machinery might turn out to be a piece of clockwork with feelings driving each other like cogwheels. But such speculation is over the horizon of current science. In the meantime if a brain announces that it has free will we might as well agree (Cairns-Smith, 1999).

Shakespeare's Iago (1605) is more subtle than his Caesar and sees the operation of free will on an extended time-scale:

> ...'tis in ourselves that we are
> thus or thus. Our bodies are gardens; to the
> which our wills are gardeners: so that if we plant
> nettles, or sow lettuce; set hyssop, and weed-up thyme;
> to supply it with one gender of herbs, or distract it with
> many; either to have it sterile with idleness, or manur'd
> with industry; why, the power and corrigible
> authority of this lies in our wills.

There are indeed about five time-scales that appear more or less explicitly in Hodgson's essay, and which are somewhat differently relevant to questions of responsibility and culpability.

1. (Unconscious) reflex: less than half a second

I have already touched on this . It raises a question: Are we responsible for actions that we do on a time-scale of under half a second? Sometimes, at least, the Law thinks so. A piece of careless driving or giving in to an impulse to slit someone's throat might happen within a reflex time scale.

2. Conscious control: seconds

This is a collaboration now between unconscious and conscious. The conscious part is at the helm, we might say, and it may take a few seconds to make changes in rudder settings and for the boat to react to them. But these small delays are of no great consequence for the overall control of navigation.

3. Deliberative: minutes, hours or more

These are longer collaborations, coming and going between unconscious and conscious: between intuition and rationalisation. They may be 'extended processes of decision making in which the likelihood of the various possibilities fluctuates significantly' (Proposition 1)

4. *Character forming: life long*

This is Iago's line, and it perhaps answers the above question about responsibility for hair trigger reflex actions. We may well be responsible — if our previous wilful actions had helped to make us what we are and had, as it were, set the triggers.

5. *(Unconscious) evolutionary: millions of years*

Whatever the effects of nurture, it is clear that evolution is part of the story of how we have come to be what we are: that some of our propensities to behave one way or another are encoded in our genes. Much or our variability of skills and character surely arises this way. But Hodgson, in Proposition 7, picks out a particular feature — the *capacity* to make choices between alternative courses of thought or action — as a constant of human nature, one respect in which 'each person is entirely the same'. This may sound odd in view of the variability of humans in other respects. There are, all the same, features that all humans share, such as the inability to synthesise ascorbic acid (and plausibly this is because we are all descended from a small population which had this deficiency). Perhaps the ability consciously to select between alternative courses depends on some combination of neurological features that was frozen in at an early stage of humanoid evolution.

References

Cairns-Smith, A.G. (1996), *Evolving the Mind* (Cambridge: Cambridge University Press).
Cairns-Smith, A.G. (1999), *Secrets of the Mind* (New York: Springer-Verlag).
Crick, Francis (1994), *The Astonishing Hypothesis.* (London: Simon and Schuster).
Dawkins, Richard (1986), *The Blind Watchmaker.* (London: Penguin Books).
Dawkins, Richard (1996), *Climbing Mount Improbable.* (New York: Norton).
Dennett, Daniel C. (1991), *Consciousness Explained.* (Boston: Little, Brown).
Glynn, Ian M. (1993), 'The evolution of consciousness: William James's unresolved problem', *Biological Reviews of the Cambridge Philosophical Society,* **68**, pp. 599–616.
Shakespeare, William (1599), *Julius Caesar*, Act II, scene ii, line 71.
Shakespeare, William (1605), *Othello*, Act I, scene iii, line 321.

HODGSON'S BLACK BOX

Thomas W. Clark

In seeking to establish the existence of what he calls a 'plain person's free will', David Hodgson adduces 8 conditions, the joint satisfaction of which would, he claims, result in our having such free will (proposition 9 asserts this conclusion). The plain persons' conception of free will, Hodgson says, is the libertarian conception, in which it is incompatible with determinism. Although what ordinary people actually believe about free will is an empirical matter in need of research, it's likely that many people (but not all) have at least a vague notion that to be free, we can't be completely determined in our acts, that the self has to be some sort of first cause to be 'ultimately' responsible and therefore justifiably deserving of praise and blame. If asked how individuals get to be first causes, most honest non-philosophers would have to concede that to them it's a mystery.

Although our plain person might subscribe to such a notion of libertarian free will, Hodgson's account of it is not, as he describes it, 'a simple and straightforward outline' that supplies easily understood justifications for libertarian freedom and so might capture the popular imagination. Rather, it's a highly speculative and scientifically radical account, involving contentious claims about quantum mechanics, evolution, consciousness, rationality, and the self, as well as conjectures about new types of natural laws (Hodgson's 'G-laws'). If we buy his arguments, Hodgson claims we'll be led to the conclusion that in addition to the determinism and randomness that science finds in nature, there also exists a heretofore undiscovered 'volitional causation', something special to human conscious agents. To establish this conclusion would amount to a scientific revolution of the first order. But because Hodgson's story is so speculative and his claims so empirically tenuous, it's not surprising that what he gives us, finally, is not a preview of a scientifically well-motivated paradigm shift, but an obscure *black box* of free will — a still-mysterious capacity of the self to somehow clinch a choice without being determined to clinch it in a particular direction.

We must evaluate Hodgson's account in the light of competing scientific accounts of human choice-making behaviour, using criteria of simplicity, completeness, empirical support, and agreement with the rest of science. How well does Hodgson's account *explain* choice-making compared with deterministic accounts? Although Hodgson may think that indeterministic free will is necessary to justify socially necessary attributions of credit, blame, reward and punishment (I don't think it is) it's quite possible that nothing in the natural world corresponds to his 'plain person's' conception of free will. I will first comment on Hodgson's claims about quantum mechanics, consciousness, rationality, and evolution, and then analyse in more detail his Proposition 7 concerning the subject and its capacity to select choices.

1. Quantum mechanics

In order to give the selecting subject two alternatives, neither of which is uniquely necessitated, Hodgson proposes quantum mechanics (QM) as the basis for the requisite indeterminism. But immediately he is forced to acknowledge that QM might supply only 'mere randomness', and that in any case it's not clear how QM indeterminacy relates, if at all, to the macro level of human behaviour. The problem here (and elsewhere) is that in order to make the self clearly, transparently responsible for a choice, Hodgson has to delineate some *mechanism or process* by which it determines the choice. But of course QM resists any mechanistic, causally transparent account precisely because it's essentially probabilistic in its predictions of behavior in the micro realm (putting aside the difficulties of macro level effects). Later (p. 5), Hodgson says that the subject's selections 'are likely to approximate to QM statistics', but then says it's an 'open question' how QM applies to conscious systems, and finally he declares that the causal role of experiences in determining choices 'can't be fully accounted for by *any* system of physical laws of general application, *even those of QM*' (emphasis added). Ultimately, the role of QM, 'perhaps together with chaos theory', in supplying indeterministic alternatives is left obscure on Hodgson's account, and so adds nothing to a scientific explanation of how people choose. This is a recurring difficulty in Hodgson's paper: he proposes that certain generally accepted processes or theories (QM, rationality, evolution) contribute to an understanding of choice-making behaviour, but in each case stops short of supplying a definitive causal story about that contribution, leaving the actual choice an explanatory black box. But of course such obscurity is what's necessary for 'volitional causation' — that which is neither random nor determined — to survive as a (pseudo) explanation of choice. The details of such causation are *necessarily* mysterious, for any transparent account of them would likely reveal that the choosing subject is, contrary to Hodgson's thesis, no exception to standard macro-level causality.

2. Consciousness

Hodgson claims that the choosing self is separate from contents of consciousness, something 'active' that is the 'bearer or experiencer of the contents of consciousness'. But recent theories of phenomenal experience, some of them well-elaborated and consistent with neuroscientific findings at many levels, suggest that the conscious self is actually one of the *contents* of consciousness (Damasio, 1999, 2000; Metzinger, 2000a,b) — a stable phenomenological *construction within experience*, not an irreducible agent/force that 'bears' or 'experiences' experience. The conscious subject, by virtue of being a construction, is not an entity or agent which could exert control over choices above and beyond those control mechanisms already instantiated by neural processes, whether conscious or unconscious, some of which constitute the sense of self. Despite the fact that Hodgson disavows a distinct mental substance or soul, he suggests an underlying dualism in claiming that the causal powers of the conscious self aren't simply those of the physical processes that correlate with consciousness. He needs this residual dualism, of course, in order to make the conscious self rule over the deterministic mechanisms of the brain. But as neuroscientific understanding of the sense of self grows, it's becoming more and more plausible that a certain sub-set of neural processes *are* the self as modeled by neural processes, e.g., those that instantiate internal representations of homeostatic functions that preserve bodily integrity (Damasio, 1999; 2000).

There is likely a range of unconscious and conscious processes involved in deliberate choices, and what Benjamin Libet's (1983) famous experiments (discussed by Hodgson) really show is that consciousness is not an uncaused, undetermined initiator or chooser, but rather an essential component of choice making that's *causally continuous* with unconscious mechanisms. Consciousness is certainly necessary for making voluntary, rational, morally responsible choices (although not all such choices involve advance deliberation, of course), but it isn't likely free in a contra-causal sense that would endow the conscious subject with 'ultimate', *'causa sui'*(Strawson, 1998) or 'interventionist' (Blackburn, 1999, ch. 3) responsibility.

On page 8 above, Hodgson argues that since pain and other phenomenal states play a causal role in mediating behaviour, and since such subjective feelings can't just *be* a matter of algorithmic computation performed by a physical substrate, there's something non-computational and non-algorithmic (namely, consciousness) playing a causal role in selecting choices. But on increasingly well-documented functionalist-representationalist accounts of phenomenal consciousness, the second premise in this argument is questionable. Hodgson overlooks the possibility that (e.g.) pain has a particular subjective feel *because* of the functional and representational roles of the neural states that constitute it — that function and feel are perhaps identical, but differently 'presented' depending on whether one occupies a first versus a third-person perspective regarding the token phenomenal pain in question (Metzinger, 2000a; 2003). So consciousness might well be computational at the right level of description.

Hodgson says (p. 10) that we should accept the first-person deliverances of consciousness as good, face-value evidence for his claims about the existence of non-algorithmic, non-rule-governed volitional causation: 'All this is confirmed by the powerful and ineradicable feeling we have that we are consciously making choices and making things happen by doing them.' But of course the feeling that something is the case can't confirm that it *is* the case, and good scientific explanations of behaviour are notorious for undermining commonsense folk psychological convictions based in untutored experience. In this instance, Daniel Wegner (2002) cautions us that we should most definitely *not* accept the feeling that 'we are consciously making choices' as evidence of anything except that we have such a feeling. The actual status of the 'we', the 'making choices', and the feeling of choice-making are matters for science, not introspection, to determine.

3. Rationality

On page 7, Hodgson says that consciously experienced reasons are essential to choice, but that they only influence, not determine, our selections. One wants to know then, what *does* determine the choice? Hodgson's thesis is that the *self* determines the choice via volitional causation, but of course such causation requires that the self can't be fully determined *itself* or determined in its choice-making, which is why on Hodgson's theory even very powerful, persuasive reasons must be 'non-conclusive' and undetermining. But, if reasons are indeed non-conclusive, then it follows there is literally no *reason* why the self reaches the choice it does — the choice is made, finally, on some other, non-reasons basis. And this basis is left obscure. As with quantum mechanics (section 1 above) and evolution (section 4 below), the role of rationality in explaining choices reaches a certain, 'non-conclusive' limit, and then hits the wall of the black box of freely willed choice, which remains frustratingly unexplained.

Despite conceding we are rational animals, Hodgson maintains there are no 'clinchers' or final determiners to be found in the operations of rationality. But of course there often *are* obvious clinchers in the various reasons that we normally cite in explaining morally responsible choices, and these stand as counter examples to Hodgson's thesis. Virtuous, law-abiding citizens often choose the way they do because they find the reasons for good behaviour e.g., maintaining their reputation among their peers, the 'benselfish' (Dennett, 2003, pp. 193–7) consequences of altruistic acts — *compelling*, and to be thus compelled is not to render good behaviour any less admirable or the agent unworthy of praise. Nor would finding out that the acts of rational evil-doers were clinched by their nefarious, abhorrent *reasons* make such acts less wrong and the agent less accountable to moral norms and the law. Rationality is the criterion of responsible agenthood precisely because it permits the agent to anticipate the consequences of an act, and our practices of holding people responsible *engage* such rationality by making certain consequences reliably contingent on behaviour (drive while drunk, lose your license). If Hodgson's black box of free will were interposed between the motivated, reasons-responsive agent and the social contingencies of our responsibility practices, such practices would have no power to shape behaviour, since after all, the agent would be ultimately free to choose a course of action that ignored whatever contingencies were in place (a point made by Pinker, 2002, p. 177). But it's manifestly the case that such practices *do* have tremendous power, that rational agents do indeed respond rationally to social norms and laws. That is, they respond in a reasons-*responsive* manner, a manner that is best explained in terms of a high-level, agent-centred, but nevertheless causal story in which the self is *not* free to ignore, on some obscure, extra-rational basis, the demands of anticipated contingencies.

On page 8, Hodgson says that 'What is often overlooked is that, apart from rules of reasoning such as those of mathematics, logic, and probability theory, there are no known rules (that is, strict rules as distinct from non-conclusive heuristics) governing good plausible reasoning.' But the formal rules of reasoning Hodgson cites are powerful rules indeed; they are at the core of logically sound argument, of deducing the implications of evidence, and of quantitative theory construction. Rational agents ignore them at peril of becoming irrational. Of course there is clearly more to embodied, real-world human rationality than formal entailment from axioms and premises, for instance those problem-solving intuitions that spontaneously arise from long-standing experience in a skill or knowledge domain. But it's not necessarily the case that what's unformalizable at the phenomenal, subject level is for that reason non-algorithmic at the machine or design level (Dennett, 1989).

Hodgson argues that

> If we cannot rely on our plausible reasoning as the conscious non-algorithmic process that we instinctively take it to be, then any confidence that we could have in it would have to depend on the circumstance that it comprises computation-like processes whose reliability is assured by the evolutionary tests they have passed; yet any belief in this circumstance and accordingly any justified confidence would itself depend on extensive plausible reasoning, giving rise to a vicious circle.

But this not-so-vicious circle can be broken simply by dropping the not-so-instinctive assumption that our reliance on reason is only warranted if it is non-algorithmic. Confidence in our reasoning powers doesn't depend, as Hodgson seems to think, on some sort of non-mechanistic, non-computable causal disconnection from the world's influence upon us. Rather, it's warranted because, by and large, we get the facts about the world right via normal perceptual and cognitive processes that reliably track the world via consistent causal channels, and we reason successfully via other processes that reliably distinguish perceived reality from our simulated internal worlds of memory, imagination, and anticipation. Any choice-making ability that allowed indeterministic slack between input and output would be *less* efficacious, *less* rational, than a system that accurately reflected, via deterministic processes, the relevant contingencies of the environment and its own self-interested agenda. Because we are entirely physical, embodied creatures, there is good reason to think that rationality and cognition are indeed instantiated by deterministic, causal processes, albeit highly ramified and perhaps only fully understood at the representational, not physical, level. But again, having the causal story go through *transparently*, from world to rational agent and back out again in cognitively adept behaviour, would reveal the agent as only the proximate, not ultimate cause of behaviour, and therefore not ultimately deserving of credit and blame. So rationality, for Hodgson, must remain causally obscure within the black box, not transparently available to science, which is why his account won't win many converts among the empirically inclined.

4. Evolution

Hodgson wants to keep his theory naturalistic, and to this end cites the evolutionary origins of our choice-making powers. But the problem he faces is that evolutionary explanations are *causal* explanations involving various mechanisms of selection that operate via discrete, more or less specifiable systems (genes, organisms, environments), and it's unclear how such a causal, mechanism-employing, rule-governed process could produce something a-causal, non-mechanistic, and non-rule governed (volitional causation). He says:

> Our rationality is well adapted to dealing with problems remote from the evolutionary tests that faced our evolutionary ancestors, and this makes it unlikely that it is no more than a matter of useful algorithmic processes selected through those tests.

How then, one wonders, *did* our purportedly non-algorithmic rationality get selected by evolution? On this question, Hodgson is notably silent. In fact, it's questionable whether the problems we deal with are really so remote from those faced by our evolutionary ancestors, and therefore questionable to suppose there must be any radical discontinuity in our cognitive powers from those possessed by our forbearers. If we drop the requirement that consciousness and rationality must be non-algorithmic and non-rule-governed (see sections 2 and 3 above), then the problem of their natural origination becomes tractable. And if we agree (as Hodgson does) that evolution — a blind, deterministic, mechanistic, purely physical process — did indeed produce our choice-making capacities, this lends considerable support to the idea that consciousness and rationality *themselves* are nothing other than a complex elaboration of deterministic, mechanistic, fully physical processes, even though it may not feel that they are.

It's also not clear how being *non-ruled governed* creatures would confer any selective advantage. As noted above in section 3 on rationality, any indeterministic slack between the influence of reasons and behavioural output would undermine, not increase, the efficacy of goal-directed action. So although Hodgson wants (understandably) to make his account consistent with one of biology's most fundamental and productive theories, the central elements of his account — *non-algorithmic* consciousness and reason — don't seem to be implied or explained by that theory. This undercuts the scientific plausibility of his thesis, especially when we compare it to mainstream neuroscientific, cognitivist and evolutionary-psychological explanations of rationality and consciousness that accept good old-fashioned causal determinism as a working assumption, and that fill in the evolutionary story behind human behaviour (e.g., Dehaene, 2002; Dennett, 2003; Pinker, 1999; Ridley, 2003). To compete against these explanations, Hodgson must explain precisely how evolution installed the black box of free will, and what indispensable function it serves, beyond supplying an ultimately responsible, buck-stopping agent.

5. Agent and selection

Of crucial importance to the plausibility of Hodgson's theory of choice is the delineation of the subject that does the choosing and the process by which the choice is made, discussed in Proposition 7. On both counts, as on other topics, Hodgson is frustratingly vague. Moreover, he vacillates about what's crucial in explaining choice: a person's specific character versus a general capacity, shared by all persons, to select choices. He says:

> The totality of 'the way a person is', prior to the selection being made, is inconclusive as between the available alternatives: it gives rise to reasons and tendencies to act in one or other of the ways that are open, but does not pre-determine the outcome.

So we ask, what *does* determine the outcome? Presumably something other than the totality of the way the person is, namely the 'capacity to select'. Regarding this Hodgson says:

> In relation to this capacity, each person is entirely the same, unaffected by differences in pre-choice states, whether due to genes, environment, prior selections, or all three; and in relation to its *exercise, to the extent that* each person can notionally be considered apart from differences affecting alternatives, reasons and tendencies, each person is entirely the same (my emphasis).

So Hodgson claims that both the *amount* and *exercise* of the capacity to select is identical across persons, unaffected by any differences in pre-choice states. But if this capacity is really identical across all persons, then the only things that can explain differences in behaviour are differences in character. Hodgson says, in fact, that

Different persons have different characters, and act differently *because* of these different characters. However, I am suggesting that this is because of the differences that pre-choice states make to alternatives, reasons, and tendencies, not because of any differences in the persons' capacity to select (my emphasis).

So the capacity to select, since it's exactly the same for all persons, really *adds nothing* to the explanation of how individuals make their choices, despite the fact that Hodgson says it alone does the selecting. It seems we need only appeal to the way the person *is*, which is what standard deterministic explanations of choices do. But for Hodgson all this useful, explanatory, predictive information about character, alternatives, motives, desires, etc. is somehow still 'inconclusive' — there's still the 'clincher' needed, that provided by the capacity to select:

> ... our particular characteristics do not *otherwise* affect the way we exercise our capacity to select. We do this [that is, we select] by choosing which alternative occurs, thus providing the clincher; and there is an element (by which I do *not* mean a distinct or severable element) of this process that is entirely up to us, unaffected by any differences between different persons. And as asserted by the fifth proposition, this does not mean that the selection, or any part of it, is random or otherwise not rational (original emphasis).

According to this passage, which seems to contradict his claim that '[persons] act differently because of these different characters', our selection of a choice is *not* determined by our character, rather our selection is *influenced, but not decided by*, the alternatives that our character brought into being prior to the selection. What finally decides or clinches the choice, is 'entirely up to us', but for Hodgson the 'us' doing the selecting is something *other* than our character, since it's something 'unaffected by any differences between different persons'. So, although Hodgson claims I am wrong to say (in Clark, 1999, p. 286) that he 'makes the choosing subject an abstract entity devoid of character and motives', it seems to me that I'm correct in this assessment, given that Hodgson's clincher has nothing to do with character, but instead derives from a capacity possessed and exercised identically across all agents.

He counters my assessment by saying: 'The subject is the unique totality of all its properties, and it is precisely because this unique totality together with particular experiences enters into the causal process that outcomes are not predetermined by constituent properties which it may share in varying degrees with other entities and with which general laws can engage.' But the unique subject that Hodgson cites here is exactly that which he claims *plays no role* in the final determination of choice, since he says the 'us' that provides the clincher is 'unaffected by differences between different persons'. The unique subject, if it is to be credited with clinching a choice, has to determine the choice, but according to Hodgson, the clincher *isn't* determined by the alternatives given by the unique subject, only *influenced* by them. The clincher is determined by a capacity identically shared and exercised by all subjects. Thus it seems my original description of Hodgson's chooser, as an 'abstract entity devoid of character and motives', is on the mark. What has free will and can be held ultimately responsible, on Hodgson's theory, has nothing to do with the real, distinguishable people that show up in court.

Note also that Hodgson wants the clincher to be rational, not random; after all, if it were random we couldn't credit or blame the agent. But rationality necessarily requires the situated subject to take into account its unique circumstances and motives in deciding a course of action. Any aspect of a subject causally disconnected from such motives and circumstances, i.e., something identical across all subjects which is merely influenced but not *determined* by such specific, situational motives and circumstances, would have, finally, no reason to clinch the choice in a particular direction advantageous to the agent. So again, Hodgson's abstract capacity for choice *adds nothing* to our understanding or explanation of how we choose; it's a disconnected, causally irrelevant cog in the choice-making mechanism, put there only to rescue the ultimately autonomous self. We do, of course, share with other agents general rational capacities for deliberation, anticipation, and recollection, but there's no reason to think that these capacities are in any way undetermined, instantiated as they are by our physical brains. And these capacities can't, of course, be Hodgson's 'element …of this process that is entirely up to us, unaffected by any differences between different persons', since people vary considerably in cognitive styles, self-knowledge, foresight, and other traits and abilities that constitute the exercise of rationality.

Conclusion

A plausible scientific account of human behaviour and choice-making must be transparent in its connections to other well-established scientific laws, principles, processes, and entities. The prospects for Hodgson's account achieving such connections are remote, given that it depends on a host of empirically tenuous claims and tentative suggestions concerning quantum mechanics, consciousness, rationality, evolution, and special laws of nature concerning choice and morality which to my knowledge have little precedent in the scientific literature (space limitations preclude my taking up the prospects for his 'G-laws').

For Hodgson, there can't be a 'conclusive' causal story explaining choices on the basis of an algorithmic rationality, personality traits, motives, external circumstances, and other determinate factors, for that would be to succumb to a determinism that shows the agent to be part of a larger causal chain, and thus not 'ultimately' responsible. To get the buck to stop at the agent, Hodgson must insert within each of us the black box of an undetermined, radically free, yet rational decision-making capacity. But it's unclear how being undetermined in any respect is compatible with being optimally rational; it's unclear how human agents are exceptions to ordinary natural causality, even in their highest deliberative capacities; and moreover we don't need to possess such black boxes — that is, to be ultimate originators — to be held compassionately responsible and accountable. Jurists and legal scholars are, under increasing pressure from the sciences, finally coming to terms with determinism, and Hodgson is bucking the tide in supposing that justice requires libertarian free will (see, for instance, Moore, 1997 and Morse, 1998; 2000). The consequences of accepting that we are indeed fully caused in our choices, although beyond the scope of this reply, may well include humane reforms in the criminal justice system (Clark, 1996; Greene & Cohen, 2004), reforms which I suspect Hodgson would support.

References

Blackburn, S. (1999), *Think* (Oxford: Oxford University Press).
Clark, T. (1996), 'The freedom of Susan Smith', *Humanist*, **56** (2).
Clark, T. (1999), 'Fear of mechanism', in Libet *et al.* (1999).
Damasio, A.R. (1999), *The Feeling of What Happens* (New York: Harcourt Brace).
Damasio, A.R., Grabowski, T., Bechara, A., Damasio, H., Ponto, L.L.B., Parvizi, J., Hichwa, R.D. (2000), 'Distinctive patterns of subcortical and cortical brain activation associated with self-generated emotions and feelings', *Nature Neuroscience*, **3** (10), pp. 1049–56.
Dehaene, S. (ed. 2002), *The Cognitive Neuroscience of Consciousness* (Cambridge, MA: MIT Press).
Dennett D. (1989), 'Murmurs in the cathedral', review of Roger Penrose's *The Emperor's New Mind* in *Times Literary Supplement*, September 29–October 5, 1989, 4513, pp. 1055–6.
Dennett, D. (2003), *Freedom Evolves* (New York: Viking Press).
Greene, J. & Cohen, J. (2004), 'For the law, neuroscience changes nothing and everything', Philosophical Transactions of the Royal Society of London (Science B), Theme issue on 'Law and the brain', 359, pp. 1775–85. Published online at: http://www.csbmb.princeton.edu/~jdgreene/Greene-WebPage_files_GreeneCohenPhilTrans-04.pdf
Libet, B., Gleason, C., Wright, W., and Pearl, D. (1983), 'Time of conscious intention to act in relation to onset of cerebral activities (readiness potential): the unconscious initiation of a freely voluntary act', *Brain*, 106, 623-42.
Libet, B., Freeman, A. & Sutherland, K. (ed. 1999), *The Volitional Brain* (Exeter: Imprint Academic).
Metzinger, T. (ed. 2000a), *Neural Correlates of Consciousness: Empirical and Conceptual Questions* (Cambridge, MA: MIT Press).
Metzinger, T. (2000b), 'The *subjectivity* of subjective experience: a representationalist analysis of the first-person perspective', in Metzinger, 2000a, pp. 285–306.
Metzinger, T. (2003), *Being No One: The Self-Model Theory of Subjectivity* (Cambridge, MA: MIT Press).
Moore, M. (1997), *Placing Blame: A general theory of criminal law* (Oxford: Clarendon Press).
Morse, S. (1998), 'Excusing and the new excuse defenses: a legal and conceptual review', *Crime and Justice*, **23**, pp. 329–406 (University of Chicago Press).
Morse, S. (2000), 'Deprivation and desert', in *From Social Justice to Criminal Justice: Poverty and the Administration of Criminal Law*, ed. Heffernan, W.C. and Kleinig, J.(Oxford: Oxford University Press).
Pinker, S. (1999), *How the Mind Works* (New York: W.W. Norton & Company).
Pinker, S. (2002), *The Blank Slate* (New York: Viking Press).
Ridley, M. (2003). *Nature Via Nurture: Genes, Experience, and What Makes Us Human* (New York: Harper Collins).
Strawson, G. (1998), 'Luck swallows everything', *Times Literary Supplement*, June, 1998, at http://www.naturalism.org/strawson.htm.
Wegner, D. (2002), *The Illusion of Conscious Will* (Cambridge, MA: MIT Press).

DO HODGSON'S PROPOSITIONS UNIQUELY CHARACTERIZE FREE WILL?

Ravi Gomatam

The plain person's view, as per Hodgson, is that free will is causally efficacious in the lived world.

Hodgson formulates nine propositions that elaborate this plain person's view of free will. He also offers detailed justifications that he hopes are philosophically and scientifically respectable. While Hodgson doesn't state anywhere what would count as a 'scientifically respectable' proposition, he seems to expect that any scientific theory of consciousness and free will must fully account for his nine propositions, not just explain them away. Or, alternatively, any scientific theory of free will that is incompatible with his nine propositions cannot serve as a possible framework for developing a scientific theory of conscious free will.

The propositions themselves, which articulate clearly the commonsense view of free will, are a good beginning, since as Einstein (1936, p. 351) has noted: 'science is nothing more than a refinement of everyday thinking. It is for this reason that the critical thinking of the physicist cannot possibly be restricted to the examination of the concepts of his own specific field. He cannot proceed without considering critically a much more difficult problem, the problem of analysing the nature of everyday thinking.'

However, on the philosophical front, I find two problems: (a) Hodgson does not justify his (correct) separation of physical and volitional will, and (b) this separation is contradictory to his claim that his view of free will is incompatible with a deterministic view of physical causation. However, I show how the separation can be philosophically justified in a manner that also avoids the contradiction stated in (b). Thus, both problems seem easily surmountable.

The task of rendering his view of free will scientific needs considerably more work. I argue that Hodgson's twin assertions about quantum theory — that quantum indeterminism is mere randomness, and that no physical theory, quantum theory included, can address the gestalt-aspect of individual experiences — are both problematic because, as I show, at least the first three of his nine propositions also apply to the quantum description of matter. I conclude by pointing out what it would take for Hodgson to make his nine propositions bear upon the *praxis* of science.

The contradiction in Hodgson's statement that his view of free will 'is explicitly inconsistent with determinism' arises in the following way. I presume he means the determinism of classical physics. Hodgson also holds that the domain of operation of physical law does not cover the domain of operation of free will. He says as much: 'I prefer to distinguish *physical causation*, which is that aspect of causation capable of being fully understood in terms of the operation of laws of nature and randomness, and *volitional causation*, in which the conscious activity of a subject or agent makes a contribution that can't be fully understood in that way' (page 16). This immediately raises a difficulty with Hodgson's position. His opening stance that his plain-person-view of free will is incompatible with the determinism of classical physics would be true only if he also considers deterministic physics to give the full story about all causation that there is. Hodgson clearly doesn't believe in this, since he thinks volitional causation is over and beyond physical causation. These two stances appear contradictory.

I, however, believe that Hodgson's separation of physical causation from the everyday notion of volitional causation can be justified by utilizing an analysis that I have given of scientific realism (Gomatam, 2004). I will summarize that analysis here and show its utility to avoid the above-mentioned contradiction.

All physical theories, in the first instance, can only correlate what we do to what we observe in the laboratory. This is true not only of quantum theory, but of even classical mechanics, as Mach showed. According to Mach, the laboratory observations are to be treated, in the first instance, as solely our outer experiences. The scientific law is nothing but a short-hand way of representing observable regularities amidst these experiences. These experiences must be interpreted using concepts closest to our experiences, namely ordinary language concepts. This is the theory of Machian sensationism (see, e.g., Mach, 1914).

Physicists, on the other hand, are realists in practice. However, scientific realism need not be seen as being opposed to Machian sensationism. Scientific realism can start with Machian sensationism as the logically necessary first step and then go beyond it. Indeed, practising physicists first describe the observational content of a physical theory in terms of ordinary language statements, and then go beyond Machian sensationism by re-interpreting the observations using the terms of the theoretical language. Thus, a quick account of the *classical* realist conception of the scientific praxis can be said to comprise the following stages.

(1) State the predictive content of the physical formalism using ordinary language, treating the laboratory observations qua our experiences. (Machian sensationism)
(2) Interpret the experiences as events in the external or real world, assuming naïve realism. (Necessary for the experimentalist's praxis)
(3) Verify the predictions.
(4) If verified, re-describe the observations using theoretical language (A statement such as 'meter needle points to +5' would become 'the value of i was measured to be +5.').
(5) Re-describe the observations using theoretical terms, but now named using words of the ordinary language. A statement such as 'the meter needle points to +5' would now become 'the value of current was measured to be 5 amperes.'
(6) Treat the value for the observed property as having existed in the world prior to and independent of the observations.

I have argued in detail elsewhere (Gomatam, 2002) that stage 5 is crucial for the physicists' claim that the *abstract* world of physics (where the dynamics of the theory takes place) is 'real', since this claim is *not* by correspondence, but by *analogy* to the real world of commonsense thinking. Briefly, in stage 5, the restatement of the scientific observations by *naming* the theoretical terms using *ordinary language words* enables the physicists to communicate the felt 'reality' of the abstract, non-sensible, physical world in terms of our only source of knowledge of the real, namely the common-sense notions of the external world in everyday experience. The ordinary language words, while naming the theoretical terms, play only a suggestive or evocative role, since the identity between the physical object and the common-sense object corresponding to its name is never perfect, only an *idealization*. Therefore, though the ordinary language words enable one to visualize the formal physical world in terms of common-sense space and time pictures, one accords the mathematical formalism itself the primacy in determining the true meaning of these terms. In this sense, the world of physics is made real only by analogy to the real world of common-sense thinking, not by correspondence. Furthermore, the world of physics is *internal* to each theory and thus is also *different* in each theory. On these counts, the world of physics cannot be directly construed as a model of the external or real world. Everyday realist thinking and scientific realist thinking, despite sharing a common realist viewpoint, meet only at the point of experience (Stage 1 above).

This means 'determinism' is a feature of the world that is *internal* to physical theory (in this case, classical mechanics) whereas, the free will of the naïve realist and everyday thinking is a feature of the real world that is *external* to physical theory. This shows why a non-deterministic and non-random free will (which operates in the real world) need not be incompatible with the determinism of classical physics (which holds in the world of physics). It also accomplishes the separation between physical causation and volitional causation that Hodgson wants.[1]

The distinction between the world of physics and the real world can also form the basis for understanding why classical physics provides answers only to 'how' type questions, whereas common-sense thinking answers 'why' type questions also. For example, if A throws a stone and breaks a window, both in classical mechanics and in common-sense thinking we provide an answer to the question 'how did the window break?' by relating the occurrence of the individual event to the picture of motion. However, the question 'why did the window break' (in the sense of why was the stone thrown in the first place) would be explainable only by using the common-sense notion of free will in terms of the volition of A. In classical mechanics, such a 'why' type question would translate to 'why are the initial conditions for the stone's motion what they are' and within classical mechanics that is a given, capable of no further explanation.

Furthermore, it is necessary to stress that even at the level of answering the 'how' type questions, the two explanations differ. Classical physics accounts for the observations in terms of the motion of point-particles in the abstract Euclidean space of mathematics, while everyday thinking would relate the observation to the motion of a macroscopic object (the stone, in this case) in the lived world. The two causal accounts have their own pragmatic utility at the level of experience, where they meet, but as already noted, at the ontological level they do not correspond to each other. If we roughly identify the physical/volition causation divide that Hodgson adopts with the how/why modes of explanation, it is not so

---

[1] Of course, this conception of the scientific realist praxis that underlies classical mechanics fails in quantum theory. However, at which stage it fails can be variously interpreted. Orthodox quantum theory, for example, regards stage 6 as failing, and thus embraces quantum contextuality: quantum mechanical properties cannot be predicated definite values except in the context of an actual measurement. Bohr placed the failure at stage 4, due to an inseparability that I discuss presently. I take the view that stage 1 itself might be seen as failing in quantum theory, in the sense that we need to invoke a different range of ordinary language vocabulary to report the observations. See Gomatam (2004) for more details.

much a matter of whether physical causality can be 'understood in terms of the laws of nature in physics', as Hodgson puts it. Rather, it is that the everyday mode of thinking involving physical causality has aided the development of causal laws in physics (such as 'determinism') that yield accurate predictions in the lived world, whereas the everyday thinking in terms of volition has not.

However, it is logically possible that even the volitional discourse in everyday thinking might aid development of theories within physics that make successful predictions in the lived world, or help understand a current physical theory that makes successful predictions but otherwise present paradoxes to our understanding. Such a development would not, upon the view presented here, undermine the efficacy of our volition at the level of everyday thinking. Therefore, it would also be compatible with Hodgson's overall view about free will. This point becomes important when we consider quantum theory.

Regarding quantum theory, as already noted, Hodgson makes two points. First, he claims, 'according to QM, any indeterminism is mere randomness' (page 4 above). However, randomness is not the only possible view of quantum theory. Causal interpretations of quantum indeterminism do exist, such as Bohm's pilot-wave theory, many-worlds, or collapse interpretations.

Hodgson's second point about quantum theory concerning our free-willed behavior arises when he says, 'whole particular gestalt experiences ... have an irreducible causal role in what happens.' I agree. He goes on to say, 'this causal role cannot be fully accounted for by any system of physical laws of general application, even those of QM' (page 9). Again, I agree. Nevertheless, quantum theory does involve a fundamental feature of inseparability and entanglement, either of the observed system with the measurement apparatus, or of pairs of distant particles in EPR-like experiments. These are holistic features, which emerge in some interpretations as physical nonlocality.

Bohr moved to avoid the consequence of physical nonlocality, but he was obliged to then treat the observed system and the observing means as a single inseparable *epistemic whole*: '... universal quantum of action expresses a feature of wholeness in atomic processes that prevents the distinction between observation of phenomena and independent behavior of the objects, characteristic of the mechanical conception of nature.' (Bohr, 1957, p. 98) He concluded, 'an independent reality in the ordinary physical sense can neither be ascribed to the phenomena *nor to the agencies of observation*' (Bohr, 1957, p. 48, italics mine).

What is not so well known perhaps is that Einstein too moved to give an epistemic reading of the psi function in order to avoid physical nonlocality, and he was also obliged to embrace a epistemic holism of another sort: Einstein held that the psi function described the state of the ensemble as a *single, logical whole*. 'The description by means of a psi function refers only to an ideal systematic totality but *in no wise to the individual system*' (Einstein, 1949, p. 669, italics mine).[2]

---

[2] Could Einstein have intended here a simple 'ensemble interpretation' in the sense of classical statistical mechanics? I do not think so since in any such statistical ensemble interpretation, the psi function

In so far as quantum theory does display a gestalt-like feature, either in the form of a physical nonlocality or an epistemic holism of the Bohr/Einstein kind, Hodgson must show in greater detail why quantum theory as it stands would not be relevant to scientifically discuss the causal role of the gestalt aspect of our individual experiences.

Hodgson's claim that quantum indeterminism is mere randomness is plausible enough, granting him certain assumptions. Quantum holism, while requiring more discussion from him, might not still oblige him to revise his stand that quantum theory does not apply to conscious systems. However, I shall now discuss a third connection that arises between quantum theory and his description of free will: the language of his first three propositions on free will can be also invoked to discuss the behaviour of quantum systems. This has substantial implications for the status of some of his propositions as unique characterizations of our conscious free will.

Let us take the simple case of a hydrogen atom with its electron in an excited stationary state E_m. According to the basic quantum postulate, the electron will go to any one of the available lower energy stationary states E_n by emitting radiation, and the physical laws only specify the statistics governing a large number of such individual transitions. This situation is compatible with the language of Hodgson's proposition 1: 'There is a pre-choice state such that the way the world is and the laws of nature leave open at least two post-choice states.' (The Alternatives Requirement). Hodgson acknowledges this.

In addition, the frequency of the radiation that the electron emits in the excited state depends, not just on the state it is in, but also on the state it will go to. Thus, as early as 1913, after reading Bohr's manuscript on the model of the hydrogen atom, Rutherford wrote back to Bohr to ask:

> There appears to me one grave difficulty in your hypothesis, which I have no doubt you fully realize, namely, how does an electron decide what frequency it is going to vibrate at when it passes from one stationary state to another? It seems to me that you would have to assume that the electron knows beforehand where it is going to stop. (Bohr, 1963, pp. 40–1)

One can raise the same question even today, with respect to the quantum mechanical model of the hydrogen atom. The question therefore remains relevant and important.

---

would represent an average state for each individual particle. Whereas, as we see in the foregoing quotation, for Einstein the psi function did not represent the state of the individual system at all, not even partially. Einstein no doubt used the word 'incomplete' to characterize quantum theory, but he defined his notion of 'incompleteness' to Schrödinger just eleven days after the publication of the EPR paper thus:

'One would very much like to say the following: Ψ stands in a one-to-one correspondence with the real state of the real system ... If this works, I talk about a complete description of reality by the theory. However, if such an interpretation doesn't work out, then I call the theoretical description "incomplete"' (Letter to Schrödinger, June 19, 1935, cited in Fine, 1986, p. 71).

Perhaps to emphasize that the rhetoric of 'completeness' in the EPR paper misses his real objection to quantum theory, Einstein later wrote: 'The (testable) relations, which are contained [within quantum theory] are, within the natural limits fixed by the indeterminacy-relation, *complete* (Einstein, 1949, p. 666, italics in the original).

To be sure, we could try to avoid the problem of having to invoke the language of choice in the above situation by choosing not to relate the observations to the individual electrons alone. This indeed is the general significance of the moves made by both Bohr and Einstein mentioned earlier. I believe the real thrust and future potential of these two epistemic approaches for an alternate realist interpretation of quantum theory without a role for consciousness have not yet been fully explored.

Hodgson's choice to see quantum mechanics as featuring an inherent randomness implies interpreting the observations in relation to the behaviour of individual electrons. Thus, already in the simple case of the hydrogen atom, Hodgson's third proposition on free will — in this transition process, the subject grasps the availability of alternatives and knows how to select one of them (the 'grasping requirement') — becomes applicable also to the behaviour of electrons as described by QT.

In proposition-2 Hodgson holds that 'the transition from a pre-choice state to a single post-choice state is a conscious process.' Given the facts that there are pre- and post-choice alternatives, and the electron does make a transition to *one* of the possible alternative states, we are left with two possible conclusions. One is to treat proposition-2 also as applicable to the behaviour of objects described by QT. This would mean quantum theory, as it stands, is a theory of consciousness and accounts for the causal efficacy of free will. But this is a conclusion that Hodgson (rightly, in my opinion) wishes to deny.

The only way out that I can see is to treat these propositions as necessary *but not sufficient* conditions for conscious free will — since the language of his first three propositions is seen to apply equally to systems described by QT.[3] With such a move, quantum theory need not involve a direct role for consciousness. I am myself inclined to the view that it is possible to develop a new, non-classical unitary ontology for matter in quantum theory without a direct appeal to consciousness. Such a new unitary ontology for matter could pave the way for a reassessment of the very issue of consciousness-matter interaction, a possibility I have discussed elsewhere (Gomatam, 1999).

In conclusion, Hodgson's stated aim — to furnish a precise formulation of the plain-person's view of free will that is philosophically and scientifically respectable — requires more work. Philosophically, I believe he commits himself (needlessly) to the stance that the determinism of classical physics is incompatible with non-deterministic, non-random free will in the lived world. This is true only if we conflate the world of physics and the 'external world' of everyday thinking via the thesis of correspondence realism which is known to have failed in physics. Once we see that the world of physics and the lived world cannot be brought into direct correspondence even in classical mechanics, we would have to ask what relevance a formulation of the notion of free will in the lived world based on common-sense notions such as Hodgson attempts could have for science. The notion of what constitutes a 'scientific proposition' has undergone a

---

[3] This is compatible with Hodgson's own limited claim that he sees his propositions as minimal requirements for conscious free will.

world of evolution, from the naïve idea that scientific statements are based on proof, to the more modest claim of Vienna verificationism, still weaker Popperian falsifiability, Feyerabend's methodological anarchism to modern-day scientific relativism and there is no consensus yet. However, a reasonable demand can be placed on Hodgson. For his account to become scientific, Hodgson must more specifically show what kind of 'formal' concepts that his propositions about the common sense notion of free will can give rise to in science, and to what kind of testable, empirical consequences they would lead. This is indeed the demand that the natural scientist is expected to place on any idea, with regard to its scientific content.

Additionally, my arguments regarding quantum theory in this commentary suggest that the implications may, in fact, run in the *reverse* direction. Quantum theory does indeed show that the first three propositions formulated by Hodgson apply equally to material systems described by quantum theory. I have proposed that by treating these propositions as necessary but not sufficient conditions for conscious free will, we could avoid directly injecting subjectivity into quantum physics. We can instead deem quantum theory as a new theory of matter that is consciousness-like. This would be compatible with the prevailing view of quantum theory as an entirely physical, albeit non-classical theory of matter. It would also mean we are yet to grasp the unique and *necessary* characteristic of consciousness in ordinary thinking. That too would be in line with the general prevailing view in 'consciousness studies' that the very nature of human consciousness remains a mystery.

The assessment that some of Hodgson's propositions are necessary but not sufficient characteristics of conscious free will need not be seen as a negative one. Elsewhere (Gomatam, 2000), I have argued that one way to render the field of 'consciousness studies' truly scientific is to make one of its primary goals precisely the identification of such necessary but insufficient conditions for consciousness. That is, let us say we identified characteristics A–Z defining conscious free will, of which some appear to be necessary but not sufficient criteria, while the rest appear to be necessary and sufficient criteria of consciousness and free will. My proposal is that in 'consciousness studies' we should be interested in the *former*, i.e. the necessary but not sufficient criteria, not the latter, since we can use the former set of criteria for developing new notions of *matter*, which would certainly be readily applicable to physics in particular and other fields of science in general. From this perspective too, I see Hodgson's efforts to be a correct first step.

References

Bohr, N. (1957), *Atomic Physics and Human Knowledge* (New York: John Wiley & Sons).
Bohr, N. (1963), *Essays 1958-1962 on Atomic Physics and Human Knowledge* (New York, London: Interscience Publishers).
Einstein, A. (1936), 'Physics and reality', *Journal of the Franklin Institute*, 221 (3), pp. 349–82
Einstein, A. (1949), 'Remarks to the essays appearing in this collective volume', in *Albert Einstein: Philosopher-Scientist*, ed. P.A. Schilpp (Illinois: Open Court); pages cited in text refer to the 1969 edition.

Fine, A. (1986), *The Shaky Game: Einstein, Realism and the Quantum Theory* (Chicago: University of Chicago Press).
Gomatam, R. (1999) 'Quantum Theory and the Observation Problem', *Journal of Consciousness Studies*, **6** (11-12), p. 173–90. Online version available at
http://www.bvinst.edu/gomatam/pub-1999-01.htm
Gomatam, R. (2000) '*What is Consciousness Studies?*' http://www.bvinst.edu/what_is_CS.htm
Gomatam, R. (2004), 'Science, philosophy and consciousness: Relearning the connections from quantum theory', in *Philosophical Consciousness and Scientific Knowledge: Conceptual Linkages and Civilizational Background*, ed. D.P. Chattopadhyaya & A.K. Sen Gupta (New Delhi: Pauls Press). Online version available at http://bvinst.edu/gomatam/pub-2004-01.pdf
Mach, E. (1914), *The Analysis of Sensations, and the Relation of the Physical to the Psychical*. Translated from the 1st German edition by C.M. Williams (Chicago: Open Court).

WHAT SHOULD WE RETAIN FROM A PLAIN PERSON'S CONCEPT OF FREE WILL?

Gilberto Gomes

Hodgson (2004) makes a forceful defence of the plain person's view that free will exists in conscious voluntary action, for which I have great sympathy. He presents arguments against the view that human action is automatically determined by external or internal factors over which the subject has no control. He contends that it is up to the person to choose among alternatives and that the person is solely responsible for her or his choices.

However, he also believes that free will is incompatible with natural causation. This is the point where I diverge from his views. In fact, both *libertarians* (such as Hodgson) who believe in a non-naturally caused free will and *determinists* who believe that free will is an illusion are *incompatibilists*. They share the view that free will is incompatible with the natural causation of conscious voluntary acts. Libertarians take side with free will and let go of natural causation. Determinists keep natural causation and relinquish freedom. *Compatibilism*, on the other hand, is the view that free will exists and is compatible with natural causation (for a review, see, for instance, Vaas, 2001). Hodgson's article may be seen as an attempt to present a 'plausible alternative to determinism'. We may say that it does not address the compatibilist alternative.

There are problems, however, with Hodgson's account. He states that it does not require the subject to 'be a 'substance' distinct from the brain processes that support it, much less an immortal soul'. He characterises it as a 'dual-aspect account of physical processes and conscious processes' (page 5 above). However, if conscious processes of free will are another aspect of physical processes of the brain, it is hard to see how they could escape being subject to physical causation.

Hodgson is not wrong in maintaining that the presence of a readiness potential (RP) prior to a conscious decision to act now is consistent with conscious free will (page 5) — even of the non-naturally caused sort that he favours. This has also been pointed out long ago by Eccles (1985), an author who, in contrast to Hodgson, does accept the existence of an immaterial self that is distinct from any brain processes and interacts with them (Eccles, 1977). Eccles (1985, p. 542) presented a hypothesis that 'preserves fully the role of conscious intention in initiating the movement'. According to this hypothesis, the earlier phase of the RP reflects spontaneous fluctuations in cortical activity, which are necessary for the immaterial agent to be able to act on the brain.

It must be recalled that the RP cannot be observed in any single EEG recording. The expression of the neural events underlying the RP is too weak to appear against the noise of neural signals registered in the EEG. It is only by averaging a large number of tracings that the RP appears. We may therefore suppose that the spontaneous fluctuations assumed by Eccles are continuously occurring, but are only detected by averaging numerous occasions in which they were seized upon by the conscious agent. The muscular movement provides in this case the zero-point from which to average the tracings backwards. When there is no movement, the spontaneous fluctuations assumed to give rise to the initial part of the RP might be there as well, but there is no way to synchronize them in different tracings so as to make them appear by averaging.

Eccles' spontaneous fluctuations in cortical activity would stand in relation to the conscious decision to act now as the sea waves stand in relation to the surfer. They are necessary requisites for surfing and can be regularly detected some time before the initiation of surfing, but they do not by themselves determine the surfer's initiation of action. If the surfer is not willing to ride on a particular wave, he or she will just let it go. However, Eccles' hypothesis is just a theoretical possibility, and we cannot see how it could be tested at present. There is no experimental evidence favouring it. On the contrary, variations in the instructions given to the subjects lead to longer or shorter RPs (Sirigu *et al*., 2003), and this goes against the idea of spontaneous fluctuations unrelated to the decision itself of when to move.

Eccles' hypothesis seems less parsimonious than the assumption that the neural processes underlying the initial RP only occur when a voluntary action is being prepared and take part in the genesis of this action. It seems that Hodgson is prepared to accept this but, according to him, these neural processes may be considered as the 'unconscious preparation [that] is required before a person has immediately available the alternatives of consciously doing or not doing an action' (page 5). Free choices would depend on a process of neural preparation which is unconscious and naturally caused. This process would do no more than present the subject with the alternatives. But why should the choice itself have to be non-naturally caused?

It seems that Hodgson is trying to salvage the plain person's intuition that a free action is determined by the conscious subject herself or himself and not by external or unconscious factors. Determinists despise the intuitions of folk psychology as prejudices that must be abandoned. I agree with Hodgson that they may instead contain valuable insights into the true nature of the mind. But is it not possible to preserve what may be good in that intuition in a way that is compatible with natural causation? I will come back to this point.

Hodgson's free will is not determined by natural laws, but he believes it can be exercised without violating those laws. He refers to quantum mechanics and chaos theory as allowing a certain degree of indeterminacy in physical events (page 9). However, neither can Hodgson's free will be accounted for by randomness. Selections are not random, they are determined by the subject's 'capacity to respond to particular gestalts' (page 11). This capacity would allow the subject to make more satisfactory choices, having thus been selected by evolution.

But it is not clear why this capacity should not be determined by natural causation. Hodgson believes that physical determinism plus randomness cannot account for 'the subject's particular gestalt experiences that are part of the pre-choice state' (page 17). Why not? One may also wonder how a capacity that is not subject to natural causality could be determined by genes (as a necessary condition for natural selection).

Hodgson argues that free choice involves rational judgment that is not accounted for by algorithmic procedures (page 8). However, being subject to natural causation does not imply that the processes leading to a free decision be algorithmic and independent of conscious judgment. Conscious judgment itself may be a naturally caused non-algorithmic process.

A compatibilist account of free will might agree with most of Hodgson's points (Gomes, 1999). We may agree that free will exists, that it involves choice among alternatives, that this choice is determined by the subject herself or himself, that free choice involves consciousness, that reasons are non-conclusive (Gomes, 2002, p. 306), that free choice is not random selection, that it may be guided by moral principles and that the subject is responsible for her or his free choices. All this may be considered as compatible with natural causation of the subject's free choices.

Of course this is a departure from the plain person's intuitive notion of a free will. But not so radical a departure as to deny the existence of free will itself. What needs to be changed is the folk concept of the subject. According to this concept, the subject acts on the world and is influenced by the world, but it is not part of the world. It is *in* the world like a fish is in the water: the fish acts on the water and the water acts on the fish but the fish is not made of water.

However, we must distinguish the *subject's* world from the *entire* world, which includes the subject. We may assume that the subject is made of the same elements and processes as the rest of the world, although it does not experience itself as being so made. We may assume that the processes that occur in the subject and determine its choices are of the same causal nature as those that occur in the rest of the world, although the subject does not experience them as such. Indeed, we may assume that the subject is a system of neural activity in a person's brain, subject to natural causation (including random processes), although this person does not experience it this way (Gomes, 1999; 2002).

According to folk concepts, if our actions are determined by natural antecedent causes they are not under our control. But why not? 'Our control' may be included in the relevant natural antecedent causes. According to folk intuition, if our actions are determined by natural causes, they are not determined by us. But why not admit that their natural causes are *in us*? According to a usual way of thinking, if our actions are subject to natural causation, then we should not bother about what to do, because it will not change anything. But why not admit that our bothering or not bothering are among the natural causes of what we do?

References

Eccles, J.C. (1977), *The Understanding of the Brain*. 2nd ed. McGraw-Hill (New York).
Eccles, J.C. (1985), 'Mental summation: The timing of voluntary intentions by cortical activity', *Behavioral and Brain Sciences*, **8** (4), pp. 542–3.
Gomes, G. (1999), 'Volition and the readiness potential', *Journal of Consciousness Studies*, **6** (8–9), pp. 59–76. Reprinted in *The Volitional Brain: Towards a Neuroscience of Free Will*, ed. B. Libet, A. Freeman & K. Sutherland (Exeter, UK: Imprint Academic).
Gomes, G. (2002), 'On experimental and philosophical investigations of mental timing', *Consciousness and Cognition*, **11**, pp. 304–7.
Hodgson, D. (2004), A plain person's free will. *Journal of Consciousness Studies*, this issue.
Sirigu, A. *et al.* (2003), 'Altered awareness of voluntary action after damage to the parietal cortex', *Nature Neuroscience*, advance online publication (30 November).
Vaas, R. (2001), Willensfreiheit. In: *Lexikon der Neurowissenschaft*. Dritter Band. Spektrum Akademischer Verlag (Heidelberg/Berlin).

ISOLATING DISPARATE CHALLENGES TO HODGSON'S ACCOUNT OF FREE WILL

Liberty Jaswal

In the sixth proposition, the proposition included for the purpose of exonerating David Hodgson's own particular account of free will from the charge of violating physical law, Hodgson fails to acknowledge and address a salient challenge that charges his account with the violation of physical law. His failure to acknowledge this is, perhaps, a result of the formulation of the objection he endeavours to resolve; and that formulation can be bolstered by confounding disparate issues, which Hodgson in fact seems to be doing.

Let us begin by stating the objection as formulated by Hodgson:

> *Unless in every case the alternatives that are possible according to QM occurs at random within the probability parameters established by the laws of QM, then physical law would be violated*, in the sense that the statistical predictions of QM would be falsified (p. 12 above, emphasis added).

It is important to take note of the emphasized segment in this formulation, for it supposes that the only challenge confronting his account is one that involves a violation of statistical predictions. Hodgson's strategy to address this challenge can be presented in two steps: first, that because of the uniqueness and complexity of pre-choice states, 'it is unlikely in the extreme' to demonstrate a 'violation of QM statistical predictions'; second, even if there were such a demonstration, it would fail to illustrate a violation of physical law because the statistical predictions that we would arrive at would not take into account certain efficaciously relevant components (p. 11 above).

Even if Hodgson is correct in his assessment above — that no violation of physical law with respect to statistical predictions can be empirically demonstrated — he entirely leaves out another possible violation. Another constraint within QM is that the character in which an event occurs must be random. Because of this, philosophers are often averse to the project of entertaining QM as a solution to the problem of free will (Searle, 2001, p. 298). This frequently noted objection found in the philosophical literature is vividly articulated by Robert Kane:

> If choices or decisions should result from [quantum uncertainties in the brain], those choices or decisions would be chance occurrences, neither predictable nor within the agent's control — more like epileptic seizures than free, responsible choices or actions.[4] (Kane, 1995, p. 125)

There is, then, this undesirable result of a free will predicated on QM, namely, the character in which the decision or action occurs must be random. Hodgson's stipulation of the character of the selection of a free choice and action is that it is non-random.[5] Therefore, Hodgson's account of free will, by its very definition, violates QM.

So that both challenges can be captured under one statement, the objection statement should be reformulated to read along the following lines: 'Unless in every case the alternatives that are possible according to QM occurs [(1)] at random [(and 2)] within the probability parameters established by the laws of QM, then physical law would be violated.' There are, evidently, at least two possible charges of violation that Hodgson's account faces. Why is it that Hodgson only acknowledges and addresses one — the statistical prediction challenge — and not the other — the randomness challenge?

Here I can only speculate as to why Hodgson does not acknowledge the other objection. There is evidence suggesting that Hodgson has confounded the statistical prediction issue with the randomness issue, i.e., that Hodgson takes there to be an equivalence relationship between the two. That is to say, Hodgson seems to suggest that if the events we observe fail to conform to their corresponding statistical predictions, then the occurrence of these events are non- random and vice versa. As for the sufficient condition for free will in the context of QM, consider Hodgson's response to Peter van Inwagen's observation that if God were to repeat several times one's pre-choice state and its corresponding post-choice state, 'the statistics of free choices [would] appear consistent with a certain probability for each decision,' and thus, free choice would seem 'indistinguishable from random occurrences within probability parameters' (p. 17 above). When Hodgson retorts, 'the statistics of many choices would not necessarily be the same as the statistics suggested by the laws of QM as applied to the pre-choice state that is

---

[4] Consider the same problem framed differently: If free will should influence quantum uncertainties in the brain, 'it would be like a nonrandom radioactive decay of atoms, a clear violation of physical laws' (Hodgson, 1999, p. 216).

[5] For the sake of the point I am trying to make I take for granted a definition of volition that is distinct from both determinism and randomness, and so we need not concern ourselves with whether or not Hodgson is successful in providing a stipulation of free choice and action that is neither determined nor random (his project of rendering intelligible the libertarian account of free will) — a project left open for others in this volume to investigate.

repeated in this way,' does he not suggest that events that deviate from their corresponding statistical predictions take on a non-random character?[6]

Not only does Hodgson seem to be assuming this sufficient condition for free will in the context of QM, but he explicitly states a necessary condition for free will in the context of QM: 'the statistics of free choices would not be the same as if free will did not exist,' i.e., if there is free will in the context of QM, then the statistics of free choice — if it could include all the relevant components — would be different from the statistics as if free will did not exist (p. 11 above).[7] By assuming this equivalence relationship between the statistical prediction issue and the randomness issue, perhaps Hodgson feels he has addressed the randomness challenge insofar as he has addressed the statistical challenge; because one cannot be true while the other false if the two are indeed equivalent, by exonerating one (the statistical prediction challenge in this case), you invariably exonerate the other (the randomness challenge in this case).

However, solving the statistical prediction issue is neither necessary nor sufficient for solving the randomness issue. To illustrate that these relationships do not hold, we need only to imagine one obtaining without the other for both directions. In the first direction, we can imagine the events that we observe deviating from their corresponding statistical predictions while the character of their occurrence remains random. Imagine that the probability parameter of the behaviour of particles under a particular set up now takes on the probability parameter, based on observations, formerly associated with the behaviour of particles under another particular set up, and vice versa. Certainly we would not conclude that the way in which the particles are now producing their actions is non-random; in fact, that they still conform to some type of probability parameter (especially in this case one formerly associated with random occurrences) is perhaps a strong indication that the character of their occurrence remains random.

In the second direction, we can imagine the statistics of free choice having the same probability parameter as that of a non-free choice. Surely if we consider the probability parameters of billions of pre-choice states if free will did exist with that of their corresponding probability parameters of pre-choice states if free will did not exist, we can imagine at least one case where the probability parameters are identical just by chance. In short, there is nothing that would prevent the possibility of the probability parameter of a pre-choice state if free will existed from being identical to the probability parameter of a pre-choice state if free will did not exist. Because it is conceivable to have the events that we observe deviate

---

[6] Indeed he does seem to be suggesting this. Since Inwagen's objection is that both the character of free choice and an ordinary quantum mechanical event are indistinguishable in the sense that they both appear random, the best interpretation of Hodgson's response to this is that he assumes that if events deviate from their corresponding statistical predictions, then they have a non-random character.

[7] There is certainly a confusion with respect to Hodgson's position on the necessary connection, or at least as far as he has articulated it, for on the one hand he writes that 'the statistics of many choices *would not necessarily* be the same as the statistics suggested by the laws of QM,' and on the other hand he writes 'the statistics of free choices *would not* be the same as if free will did not exist' (emphasis added pp. 10, 6 above).

from their corresponding statistical predictions and for those events to continue to have a random character, and for the statistics of free choices to conform to the statistics in that same case if free will did not exist, solving the statistical prediction issue is neither necessary nor sufficient for solving the randomness issue. Since the statistical prediction and randomness issues are disparate, one cannot be addressed by means of the other.

At most what the explication of proposition six does is justify why a free choice might deviate from our statistical prediction, for the statistical prediction would not take into account all the efficaciously relevant components. It does not, however, go further and defend Hodgson's account from the randomness challenge. Whether Hodgson's failure to acknowledge and address the randomness challenge is a result of confounding the issues (as I have suggested) or not does not alter the task before Hodgson — to address the randomness challenge if he is to exonerate his account of free will from the charge of violating physical law.

References

Hodgson, David (1999), 'Hume's mistake', in *The Volitional Brain: Towards a Neuroscience of Free Will*, ed. B. Libet, A. Freeman & K. Sutherland (Exeter, UK: Imprint Academic).
Kane, Robert (1995), 'Two kinds of incompatibilism', in *Agents, Causes, & Events: Essays on Indeterminism and Free Will*, ed. Timothy O'Connor (New York: Oxford University Press).
Searle, John R (2001), *Rationality in Action* (Cambridge: MIT Press).

FREE AGENCY AND LAWS OF NATURE

Robert Kane

Since the late 1970s, I have been developing and defending an incompatibilist or libertarian theory of free will that has many affinities with the view of Hodgson's paper. In my first book on free will (Kane, 1985), I defended a number of key theses of his paper, including the role of plausible reasoning and non-clinching 'incommensurable reasons' in free choice (his 'reasons' and 'selection' requirements, propositions 4 and 5), the role of consciousness in the transition from pre- to post choice states (proposition 2), the idea that libertarian free will does not require 'contra-causal' freedom or the violation of physical laws (proposition 6), the idea that ultimate responsibility is compatible with indeterminism (proposition 9), as well as his 'alternatives' (1), 'grasping' (3), and 'capacity to select' (7) requirements. That 1985 book was the first attempt to show in a detailed way how these diverse theses among others could be woven into a libertarian theory of free will that was consistent with current scientific knowledge.

So there is much that Hodgson and I agree on. (He himself has noted agreements in our views, along with some disagreements, in Hodgson 1999 and 2002). But to accept the basic propositions of his paper (which I believe are required for any coherent libertarian view) is not necessarily to accept all the arguments used in defence of them; and I have reservations about a number of arguments Hodgson uses in this paper to defend his basic propositions — reservations that I think will be shared by his non-libertarian critics. I will focus on three topics where these reservations arise: (1) the nature of *agent causation*, (2) the relation of free choice to *physical laws*, especially quantum physical laws and (3) the *randomness objection* to libertarian free will. My reservations on these topics are best understood against the background of a (necessarily brief) sketch of my own picture of undetermined free choice.

On my view, not all acts done 'of our own free wills' have to be undetermined. Many such acts can flow determinately from our characters and motives (our wills), so long as the wills from which they flow were formed in part by us by some earlier acts that were undetermined. I believe such undetermined 'self-forming' acts occur at difficult times in our lives when we are torn between competing visions of what we should do or become; and these acts are more common than we think.

Perhaps we are torn between doing the moral thing or acting from ambition or between present desires and long-term goals, or we are faced with difficult tasks for which we have aversions. In all such cases, we are faced with competing motivations and have to make an effort to overcome temptation to do something else we also strongly want. At such times, there is tension and uncertainty in our minds about what to do that, I suggest, is reflected in appropriate regions of our brains by movement away from thermodynamic equilibrium — in short, a kind of stirring up of chaos in the brain that makes it sensitive to micro-indeterminacies at the neuronal or synaptic levels. The uncertainty we feel at such soul-searching moments of self-formation is thereby reflected in the indeterminacy of our deliberative neural processes themselves. What is experienced phenomenologically as uncertainty corresponds physically to the opening of a window of opportunity that temporarily screens off complete determination by influences of the past.

The indeterminacy thus stirred up and chaotically amplified into our deliberative processing appears as background noise hindering our efforts to make either of the competing choices (moral or self-interested, prudential or imprudent, etc.) that we may want to make for different and incommensurable reasons. The indeterminism that makes it less than certain that we will make one of the choices is produced by the competing reasons and motives for making the other choice, and vice versa. As a consequence, the indeterminism affecting our deliberative processing lowers the probability that either choice will be made from what it would have been *if there had been no competing reasons*. When we do succeed in making one choice rather than the other, it will be by overcoming this hindrance.

Since the role of the indeterminism is thus to hinder the occurrence of the effect, whichever choice is made, the indeterminism is not the *cause* of the choice that is actually made. This follows from a general point about probabilistic causation. A vaccination may hinder or lower the probability that I will get a certain disease, so it is causally relevant to the outcome. But if I get the disease despite it, the vaccination is a not a cause of my getting the disease, though it was causally relevant. The causes of my getting the disease are those causally relevant factors (such as the infecting virus) that significantly raise the probability of its occurrence. In the case of the choice I do make, its causes are those causally relevant factors that significantly raise the probability of making *that* choice from what it would have been if they had not been present, such as my reasons and motives for making that choice rather than the other, my conscious awareness of these reasons and my deliberative efforts to overcome the temptations to make the contrary choice. (I appeal to parallel processing in the brain to show how such causes may be operative *whichever choice is made* [see Kane 1999, 2002]).

Finally, since the causally relevant factors that are the causes of the choice are *my* reasons, *my* conscious states and *my* deliberative efforts, we can also say that I (the agent) am the cause. The choice is not random, because it is consciously made either way for reasons, deliberately and voluntarily, and because, while chance played a role in it, chance was not its cause. I am its cause by virtue of my reasons and my deliberative efforts, which overcame the interfering effects of the indeterminism produced by the conflicting motives. The reasons were 'non-conclusive' in the sense that I could have made the alternative choice for the competing reasons. But the choice is rational nonetheless, since reasons do not have to be conclusive in that sense for choices to be rational. (Thus, I agree with Hodgson's proposition 4).

1. Agent causation

In the light of this sketch, let us look at the three topics of Hodgson's paper mentioned earlier. In a footnote in which he compares his view with mine, Hodgson says 'my view may be closer to the standard agent-causation view [held by many libertarians] than is that of … Kane.' If this is correct, then we have significant disagreements about the nature of agent causation that need to be aired. According to the 'standard agent-causation view' to which he refers, in order to make sense of libertarian free will (as something other than mere randomness), one must postulate a special *sui generis* kind of causation by a substance or agent that cannot be adequately spelled out in terms of causation by processes and states of the agent of any kinds, physical or mental. (I follow C.D. Broad in calling this a 'non-occurrent' causation, where 'occurrences' cover such things as states of affairs, processes and events.) This is a very strong claim. It is stronger than the claim that libertarian free choices cannot be adequately explained in terms of *physical* causation alone, as Hodgson claims for his *volitional* causation. I agree with that claim. To adequately explain free will one must also invoke causation by mental (including volitional) states and processes, such as reasons, motives, intentions, efforts, conscious states of awareness, deliberative processes, and so on, as in my sketch.

But standard agent-causationists go further than this. They say, not only that you cannot adequately explain libertarian free choice by invoking causation by physically-described states and processes, but you cannot adequately explain libertarian free choice when you add to physical causation, causation by mental states and processes, such as reasons, states of consciousness, and the like. To adequately answer the 'randomness' and ' luck' objections against libertarian free will, they say, you need in addition a special non-occurrent causation by a substance that is something over and above causation by physical *or* mental states and processes. I strongly disagree with this claim. Nor can I see that anything Hodgson says about his volitional causation requires a non-occurrent causation of the kind that agent-causationists invoke.

As I see it, libertarians have more than enough burdens to bear trying to make their view plausible. One of these burdens is making sense of causation by mental states and processes, or *mental causation* so-called (currently a heated topic of discussion among philosophers of mind). Libertarians should not, and need not, bear the additional burden of having to make sense of a kind of causation that is entirely beyond causation by states and processes of any kinds, physical or mental. The important thing about mental causation (as I emphasized in Kane 1985 and 1996) is that even the chief opponents of libertarianism — i.e., compatibilists — must invoke mental causation to explain free actions in compatibilist terms. I know of no prominent compatibilist account of free action or will that does not also invoke causation by reasons, desires, intentions, states of consciousness, and the like. So, by invoking mental causation, libertarians are not taking on ontological burdens that their chief opponents on free will must not also bear. Not so with the non-occurrent causation of agent-causationists. It is a new ontological kind of causation specifically invoked to salvage libertarian intuitions. I do not think it is needed for this purpose.

I suspect that Hodgson thinks his view may be closer to the standard agent-causationist view than mine because of the role that conscious states and gestalt experiences play in his view. He views conscious states and gestalt experiences as holistic in some fundamental sense and thus influencing free choices as 'whole particular experiences.' I do not deny that this is so. Such an assumption is certainly consistent with the sketch of free choice I gave earlier. But it does *not* amount to *non-occurrent* causation of the kind postulated by agent-causationists. An agent's particular conscious states or processes and gestalt experiences, whether viewed holistically or not, are still *states* and *processes* of the agent; and causation by them is causation by mental states and processes, not causation of a non-occurrent kind.

To reject non-occurrent agent-causation is not of course to deny that agents *cause* their free choices and other free acts. As noted in my sketch, to say (I) 'The agent's-being –in-certain-mental-states (such as being consciously aware of reasons) and engaging-in-certain-mental-processes (such as deliberating about what to do or making conscious efforts) causes or brings about a free choice to A' is consistent with saying (II) 'The *agent* causes or brings about the free choice to A.' Indeed, as I see it, I entails II, though the converse does not hold. I is a more informative way of asserting II. We do not have to make a choice therefore between causation by states or processes and causation by agents (as Hodgson rightly notes at one point); there is no opposition between the two.

I have always suspected that behind standard agent-causationist views is the residual fear that the 'agent' will somehow disappear from the scene if we describe its capacities and their exercise, including free will, in terms of states and processes. (Agents will disappear in the 'flux' of events.) But this fear is misguided. A continuing substance, such as an agent, does not absent the ontological stage just because we describe its continuing existence — its *life*, if it is a living thing — including its capacities and their exercise, in terms of states of affairs and processes involving it. One needs more reason than this to think that there are no continuing substances or that agents do not cause things, only events cause things. I suspect from much of what he says that Hodgson would agree with these claims. So I wonder in what respect, if at all, his view is agent-causationist in the standard sense. If the goal is to make libertarian free will consistent with scientific knowledge, we should not introduce *sui generis* forms of causation if we do not have to.

2. The relation of free will to physical laws

Hodgson says in his proposition 6 that the exercise of libertarian free will on his account involves 'no violation of physical law.' But he muddies the waters in the subsequent commentary on proposition 6, where he says the following: 'Because of the uniqueness and particularity of the [conscious] experiences' of particular subjects, the 'causal role [of these experiences] cannot be fully accounted for by any system of physical laws of general application, even those of QM [quantum mechanics]. Indeed, my suggestion is that the capacity to respond to particular gestalts...makes satisfactory choices more likely than they would be if choices occurred at random in accordance with QM statistics.' This passage seems to imply that if free choices in his sense occur, the activity of the brain must deviate, not only from deterministic laws, but from the statistical laws of quantum physics as well. This is a very strong claim; and it is not obvious how it squares with his claim in proposition 6 that libertarian free will on his account involves 'no violation of physical law.'

Hodgson responds by saying that the supposed deviation from QM statistics when free choices occur would not be a violation of (quantum) physical laws, but rather a 'limitation on their applicability' (I, 6) But this seems a mere verbal maneuver that does not get to the heart of the problem. Whether we describe the deviation from quantum statistics as a violation of quantum laws or a limitation on their applicability, the significant claim is that libertarian free choices must fail to conform, not only to deterministic laws, but to the statistical laws of quantum physics as well. To make sense of libertarian free will, we must suppose that the laws of physics, whether they are deterministic or statistical, have 'limited applicability.' It is possible of course that new laws might supersede the current laws of physics. But these new laws will presumably be either deterministic or statistical. Perhaps the new laws of physics will not specify precise statistical regularities. Perhaps they will be vague laws. Or perhaps they will have limited applicability and not apply to conscious experiences in the brain at all. But now the speculative assumptions required for libertarian free choice are multiplying. Libertarianism can be made consistent with science, but it must be a science unlike anything we currently know. One begins to hear the echo of the old familiar charge against libertarianism by P.F. Strawson that — try as they may — libertarians cannot avoid engaging in 'panicky metaphysics.'

Libertarians, of course, have a long history of claiming that free choices and actions must escape the 'clutches' of physical laws of nature. If we have free will, they have assumed, the laws of nature must have limited applicability to human behavior. Hodgson seems to be operating in this traditional mold, despite his claim in proposition 6 that libertarian free choices involve 'no violation of physical law.' Interestingly enough, compatibilists and other critics of libertarian free will often make the same assumption: They assume that free actions in the libertarian sense are only possible if physical laws of nature do not apply universally to human behavior. That is why it is assumed in many textbook discussions of free will that if you want an account of free action that is consistent with science, your only option is to be a compatibilist. The assumption that seems to me to be wrong on both sides of this debate is that libertarian freedom is possible only if physical laws of nature do not apply universally to human choice and action. My earlier sketch of libertarian free choice involves no such assumption. It does assume that the physical laws governing the activity of the brain are not all deterministic; and that is a heavy enough assumption for libertarians to bear. But that is the assumption they must bear and no more.

3. The randomness objection

Hodgson also appeals to the limited applicability of physical laws, including quantum laws, in his response to the randomness objection to libertarianism (II, 2). He considers the so-called 'rollback' version of the randomness objection, as stated by van Inwagen. Suppose God rolls back the universe many times to a person's pre-choice state. The decision (in accordance with libertarianism) sometimes goes one way, sometimes the other. But 'as the repetitions continue, the statistics of the choices appear consistent with a certain prior probability for each decision' suggesting that free choices 'are thus indistinguishable from random occurrences within probability parameters.' Hodgson responds that 'on my account ... the statistics of many choices would not necessarily be the same as the statistics suggested by the laws of QM as applied to the pre-choice state that is repeated in this way.' So the objection that the choices are 'indistinguishable for random occurrences within probability parameters' fails. Thus, the randomness objection is rejected by appealing once again to the limited applicability of quantum laws.

My view is that the randomness and rollback objections can be answered without such speculations about deviation from, or the limited applicability of, quantum physical laws. The statistical regularities applied to the pre-choice state on each rollback represent prior *propensities* of the agent to make one or another choice. But these propensities merely incline the agent to one choice rather than another (as Hodgson rightly says); they do not constrain or determine which choice will be made in the particular case. I have argued elsewhere that these propensities represent the relative strength or weakness of the agent's will with respect to the choices at hand; and these can change over time. But they do not determine the individual choice. Sometimes the strong-willed person can fall to temptation and make the imprudent choice and sometimes the weak-willed person can succeed in overcoming temptation and make the prudent choice.

There is a temptation to think that as God rolls back to the pre-choice state more and more times, the agents become more constrained by the statistical laws. We may have the feeling that if the thousandth run came up and van Inwagen's thief had robbed the poor box 499 times and refrained 500, then somehow on the thousandth run, he had to rob the poor box to even things up or that he was somehow more constrained to rob the poor box. But this is a confusion related to the gambler's fallacy. The thousandth run is no different than the first run. If the prior propensities were .5/.5 (or .6/.4 or whatever) in the original choice situation, then they are the same on the thousandth run as well and every other run; and it will still be up to the agent's deliberate and voluntary choosing to determine which choice will be made each particular time in accordance with the earlier sketch. Suppose God tired of this exercise and quit after a thousand rollbacks. Suppose also that the prior propensities for the competing choices were prudent .6/ imprudent .4 and suppose the agent had made the prudent choice 640 times and the imprudent choice 360 times. Would this mean the statistical law (that predicted .6/.4) was violated? Not at all. Statistical laws are not violated in the short run; and individual choices are short run — as short run as you can get. The fact of long-run convergence entails no *further* constraints than those involved in the existence of the prior propensities; and those propensities merely incline, they do not necessitate particular outcomes.

One certainly has to appeal to more than quantum theory to account for libertarian free will. One also needs other new scientific developments, such as complexity theory, chaos, non-linear thermodynamics, connectionist neural networks, parallel processing (all of which play a role in my account of free will). But neither does one have to suppose that these additional scientific developments require violation of basic physical laws, including quantum laws. These scientific developments do entail that novel capacities emerge as complex physical systems evolve, but the emergence of such new capacities is evidence of the astonishing fecundity of laws of nature, not of the limitations of their applicability.

In summary, I concur with most of the nine propositions that Hodgson defends in support of his 'plain person's free will'. But I have been arguing that you do not have to suppose there is a special kind of non-occurrent agent-causation or that the activity of the brain fails to conform to the laws of quantum physics to satisfy those propositions.

References

Hodgson, David (1999), 'Hume's mistake', in *The Volitional Brain: Towards a Neuroscience of Free Will*, ed. B. Libet, A. Freeman & K. Sutherland (Exeter, UK: Imprint Academic).

Hodgson, David (2002), 'Quantum physics, consciousness and free will', in *The Oxford Handbook of Free Will*, ed. Robert Kane (Oxford: Oxford University Press).

Kane, Robert (1985), *Free Will and Values* (Albany NY: SUNY Press.

Kane, Robert (1996), *The Significance of Free Will* (Oxford and New York: OUP).

Kane, Robert (1999), 'Responsibility, luck and chance: Reflections on free will and indeterminism.' *Journal of Philosophy*, **96**, pp. 217–40.

Kane, Robert (2002), 'Neglected pathways in the free will labyrinth', in *The Oxford Handbook of Free Will*, ed. Robert Kane (Oxford: Oxford University Press).

SCIENCE VERSUS REALIZATION OF VALUE, NOT DETERMINISM VERSUS CHOICE

Nicholas Maxwell

I find myself in sympathy with much of David Hodgson's beautifully lucid account of the plain person's conception of free will, but at the same time, paradoxically, out of sympathy with some quite basic presuppositions of his account. I am wholly in sympathy with his dual-aspect view of consciousness, the centrality of consciousness for free will, his anti-reductionism, his rejection of the claim that Libet's results undermine free will, and his reasons for that rejection. But I am out of sympathy with Hodgson's presupposition, apparent in the first paragraph of the article, that a central issue is whether free will is, or is not, compatible with determinism. I am out of sympathy with the way Hodgson characterizes free will as the capacity to choose. And I am out of sympathy with the incompatibilism of Hodgson's conception of free will — incompatibilism as it should be understood, namely incompatibility of free will with our scientific picture of the universe — even though just this point is denied by Hodgson.

I begin with a few remarks about how, in my view, the free will problem should be formulated.

First, I find it quite extraordinary that the entire tradition of philosophical debate about free will tends to take it for granted, as Hodgson does too it seems, that the central issue is whether free will is, or is not, compatible with determinism. The proper way to formulate this part of the problem is rather: Is free will compatible with what modern science tells us about the universe, and ourselves as a part of the universe? Or rather: Given that one can distinguish a range of conceptions of free will increasingly worth having, which of these, most worth having, is compatible with science? What of value does science permit, and what does it disallow?

The real threat to free will comes from the possibility that the universe really is as modern physics ultimately conceives it to be - physically comprehensible, that is such that some as-yet undiscovered, unified physical theory of everything in principle (not of course in practice) predicts and explains all phenomena, including all phenomena associated with human life. (For a sustained argument to the effect that we should indeed interpret modern science as telling us that the universe is physically comprehensible see Maxwell, 1998.) The nightmare possibility is that everything that we experience, think and do accords with a purely physical explanation which refers to physical entities, forces and states of affairs, but which makes no mention whatsoever of our intentions, desires, decisions. Formulating the problem in terms of determinism is too narrow because the universe, though physically comprehensible, may well not be deterministic: this may be what quantum theory, and cosmic spontaneous symmetry breaking events (if they exist) are trying to tell us. Formulating the problem in terms of determinism is too broad, because even if determinism is true, this does not mean that the universe is physically comprehensible. The universe might be deterministic, and yet the true theory of everything might be horrendously disunified and, to that extent, non-explanatory. Thus the traditional way of posing the problem gets things seriously out of focus. I say this because, to repeat, serious philosophical issues arise because of what *modern science* seems to be telling us about the nature of the universe, and ourselves as a part of the universe, and not because of what *determinism* might tell us, the latter neither implying, nor being implied by, the former. We should refer to the free will/physicalism problem rather than the free will/determinism problem - physicalism being the thesis that the universe is physically comprehensible. Habit, not thought, it seems to me, is behind the problem continuing to be construed as the free will/determinism problem.

Secondly, a few remarks about how to characterize free will.

As I have already indicated, there are, no doubt, a number of different conceptions of free will, some more worth having than others. In order to solve the free will/physicalism problem we need to know what is the most worthwhile, the most valuable, conception of free will that we can have that is compatible with physicalism. One possibility is to characterize free will, not as the capacity to choose, but rather as *the capacity to realize what is of value in a range of circumstances* — 'realize' meaning both 'apprehend' and 'make real' (Maxwell, 1984, 273–4; 2001, 149). I am delighted to see that Daniel Dennett has recently declared that 'this is about as good a short definition of free will as could be' (Dennett, 2003, p. 302). This way of characterizing free will has the following advantages. First, free will in this sense is clearly a capacity that it is supremely of value to possess. Secondly, this characterization of free will makes explicit that value judgements are relevant to assessments of free will. Thirdly, characterizing free will in this way seems to me superior to characterizing it in terms of the capacity to choose, in that choosing is neither necessary nor sufficient for free will (in a genuinely worthwhile sense) unless one means something rather special by 'choosing'. It is not necessary: we are often freest, it seems to me, when we act instinctively, spontaneously, without any explicit, conscious thought being given to which of two or more choices we make. A person instinctively, spontaneously, consoles a friend because of some grievous loss; another, a great artist, Mozart perhaps, in the full flood of inspiration, instinctively, spontaneously, creates a great work of art. Both are expressions of free will, both involve the realization of that which is of value, neither involves conscious deliberation between alternatives. What free will requires is that we *can* deliberate about what to do when we get into difficulties; but if we never act instinctively, without such deliberation, if we always deliberate before we act, our freedom is compromised, deliberation has become repressive and obsessive.[8] On the other hand, choosing is not sufficient: a lunatic who spends hours

---

[8] All achieving of what is of value is aim-pursuing, of course, and all aim-pursing, whether human, animal or robotic, requires that actions can be appropriately adapted to circumstances so that the pursued aim can be achieved in a variety of circumstances. In this 'compatibilist' extended sense of choice, all

deliberating as to which of two buttons he should press when nothing whatsoever depends on the choice would not ordinarily be said to be exercising free will, precisely because, although there is choice, the element of value is lacking. Finally, the above characterization of free will has the great advantage that it is clear from it that free will is something that can grow and diminish, because the range of circumstances in which what is of value is realized can grow or diminish, and because the value of what is sought can grow or diminish. This characterization highlights, as Hodgson's, perhaps, does not, the fundamental issue of the *growth*, the *enhancement*, of free will.

This characterization of free will does not prejudge the question of whether free will is compatible with physicalism (or determinism). Incompatibilists may (and will) argue that nothing of value is realized without the capacity to choose between alternatives in a way which contradicts physicalism (or determinism). It may be that Hodgson's conception is closer to the plain person's conception, but that does not seem to me, in itself, an advantage. No physicist would argue for the superiority of his theory on the basis that it is closer to the plain person's conceptions, and I do not think that philosophers should argue along those lines either.

It may be objected that questions about free will come up most acutely in courts of law, when what is at issue is whether a crime, an act that is evil, has been performed freely, and not an act that has as its outcome something of value. But the capacity to realize what is of value can of course be misused: in judging whether a crime was performed freely, we are judging, according to the conception of free will indicated above, whether (or to what extent) the criminal act was the outcome of the use, the dreadful misuse if you like, of the capacity to realize what is of value. A person acts without freedom to the extent that he lacks the capacity to realize what is of value. Again, it may be objected that a person may achieve what is of value unintentionally, by accident as it were, and even when acting under compulsion: this surely should not qualify as free action. But this objection can be met by stipulating that the phrase 'the capacity to realize what is of value' refers to intended value, value that is the aim of actions performed.

Despite its brevity and other advantages, characterizing free will as the capacity to realize what is of value suffers from the disadvantage that it is likely to be judged to be too different from what is ordinarily meant by free will to be acceptable. The capacity to realize what is of value depends enormously on talent, skill, education, training: but we would not ordinarily say that free will depends on such things. The capacity to realize what is of value might be called not *free will*, but *wisdom*, which is also what I have called it elsewhere (Maxwell, 1984, p. 66; 2001, pp. 149–50). Free will, it may be objected, is an altogether cruder, more basic notion; its exercise does not require such things as talent, skill or education.

The ordinary meaning of free will is captured more successfully, perhaps, by the idea that we are free if our authentic self is in control of our inner and outer actions. Our *self* is that aspect of our being — that aspect of our brain structure and function (we may assume) — which (a) controls our actions so that we act in

---

achieving of value — indeed all human action — involves choice. But this is hardly what 'choosing' ordinarily means; it is certainly not what 'choosing as a result of conscious deliberation' means.

ways characteristic of who we are; (b) specifies our basic desires, fears, hopes, goals; (c) contains a representation of the life we are living; (d) encodes memories, knowledge, and skills essential to acting as the person we are; (e) is everything experiential that corresponds to this. Consciousness is a proper part of our self, so construed. Our *authentic* self (our soul) is the self that does the best justice to our history and to what is of most value about us, the life we are leading, and our future. Our authentic self may cease to be in command if we become brainwashed, subservient to another, mad, swallowed up in some creed or movement, or overwhelmed by some obsession, powerful emotion, or craving. What does it mean to say that our authentic self 'is in control'? It means that there is a true personalistic explanation of our inner and outer actions which is such that these actions are correctly explained as being produced and guided by the authentic self in the given environment. *Personalistic explanations* of another's actions are acquired by imagining one is the other person, with the other's feelings, desires, experiences, problems, beliefs, values: see Maxwell (1984, pp. 183–9, 264–75; 2001, 103–12). Personalistic explanation is somewhat similar to 'empathic' understanding, or what psychologists call, sometimes dismissively, 'folk psychology'. We only genuinely possess free will, it may be argued, if true personalistic explanations, which explain our actions as being produced and guided by our authentic self, are not, even in principle, reducible to physical explanations (even though they are compatible with physical explanations). I have defended compatibilism along these lines elsewhere (Maxwell, 2001, chs. 5–7).

Let us call the characterization of free will as the capacity to realize what is of value 'free will$_1$', and the characterization in terms of the authentic self being in control 'free will$_2$'. Free will$_2$ has most of the virtues of free will1. Free will$_2$ is clearly something that it is of value to possess; it makes explicit the role of values (via 'authenticity'); it allows that we may be acting freely when we act spontaneously and instinctively; and it does not prejudge the free will/physicalism problem, in that incompatibilists may argue that the authentic self can only be in control if the self's control violates physical law. The two notions are related: free will1 presupposes free will$_2$, since if we suffer the loss of our authentic self, the value of everything we may realize is, for us, degraded. What shall it profit a man if he gain the whole world and suffer the loss of his own soul? However, if we take seriously the point made above that the free will/physicalism problem requires that we try to discover the most worthwhile conception of free will that we can have that is compatible with physicalism, then this implies that we should give priority to the free will$_1$/physicalism problem rather than the free will$_2$/physicalism problem — or, as we might call it, the 'wisdom/physicalism' problem.

I have another, more general reason for holding that this is the proper way to formulate at least an important part of the free will problem. Putting it this way makes clear that the free will problem is an important part of our most general, fundamental problem, not just of philosophy, not just of inquiry, but of all of life.

Elsewhere (Maxwell, 2001, ch. 1) I have argued that this most fundamental problem can be put like this: How can that which is of value associated with human life (or sentient life more generally) exist embedded in the physical universe? This is the fundamental *conceptual* problem (How is it possible for that which is of value to exist embedded in the physical universe?). It is the fundamental *theoretical* problem of knowledge and understanding (How precisely, and in detail, is that which is of value embedded in the physical universe?). And it is the fundamental *practical* problem of living (How can that which is of value be realized in this physical universe?). Theoretical physics, cosmology, biology, social inquiry, the humanities and the technological sciences deal with diverse aspects of these problems. For each one of us, the practical version of the problem becomes: How can I (or we, assuming one is living, or doing things, with others) realize what is of value in the universe to me (or to us, or to those on behalf of whom we act)? Elsewhere I have argued that the *practical* version of the problem is the most fundamental intellectually, and in order to do justice to this point we need to bring about a revolution in the aims and methods of academic inquiry: see Maxwell (1984).

The problem of free will (properly formulated as the problem of whether, or to what extent, the capacity to realize what is of value is compatible with what modern science tells us about the universe) is an important part of the above fundamental *conceptual* problem. Versions of the free will problem arise also as parts of the fundamental *theoretical* and *practical* problems — the practical problem of how we can set about *enhancing* our free will — or wisdom — being, indeed, the most basic and important.

Do these questions about how to formulate the free will problem really matter? They do. It may be too much to ask of philosophy that it should *solve* our fundamental problems, but it is not too much to ask that it should at least perform the crucial preliminary step of *formulating* our fundamental problems correctly. The entire tradition of philosophy since Descartes has failed lamentably to perform even this first step correctly, analytic philosophy being almost the worst offender. This is the case, at least, if what I have said three paragraphs up about what our fundamental problems are is correct. We need a revolution in philosophy, so that the above fundamental problems become intellectually fundamental to philosophy. This would involve philosophy devoting itself to helping to bring about a revolution in the whole academic enterprise, so that it takes as its basic task to help humanity improve its solutions to the problems of realizing what is of value in the universe as revealed to us by science. The fundamental aim of academic inquiry would become not just to acquire knowledge, but to promote wisdom by rational means. And as for free will, the central problem would be not 'Is free will compatible with determinism?' but rather 'How can free will, construed as the capacity realize what is of value in life, be enhanced?'. Philosophy quite generally, and philosophical work on free will specifically, could make a quite different and far more valuable contribution than that which academic philosophy makes at present.

I would have liked to see some hints of these issues in David Hodgson's piece on free will — although I admit that it is not quite right for me to criticize him for failing to write what he clearly had no intention of writing in the first place.

I conclude with two critical remarks concerning Hodgson's plain person's conception of free will.

First, a remark about Hodgson's claim that his plain person's conception of free will is compatible with science, at least to the extent of not involving 'a violation of physical law'. There are two very different ways in which physics may be limited in principle when it comes to explaining free human actions. First, physics provides (in principle) a (perhaps probabilistic) physical explanation for all physical processes associated with human actions but fails to explain what goes on as *intelligible human actions* — personalistic explanations, which are required for this, being non-reducible to physical explanations. Second, associated with free human actions, physical events occur which cannot be fully explained *physically* (in a possibly probabilistic way) but can only be explained by an appeal to the conscious agent. The first kind of limitation yields a compatibilist conception of free will, while the second yields a conception that deserves to be called 'incompatibilist', despite Hodgson's remarks to the contrary. Hodgson defends the second, incompatibilist conception, as his discussion of proposition 6 makes clear. This position seems to me wildly implausible. It means that evolutionary processes lead to physical events occurring which are physically inexplicable, but explicable in terms of sentient or conscious agents (which amounts to a form of vitalism). Very much to be preferred, in my view, is the first, compatibilist conception, defended in Maxwell (2001, chs. 5–7).

Second, I am not convinced that Hodgson has said enough to show that his incompatibilist conception of free will is more worth having than compatibilist versions of free will$_1$ or even free will$_2$ (Maxwell, 2001, chs. 5–7).

References

Dennett, Daniel (2003), *Freedom Evolves* (London: Allen Lane).
Hodgson, David (2004), 'A Plain Person's Free Will', *Journal of Consciousness Studies*, this issue.
Maxwell, Nicholas (1984), *From Knowledge to Wisdom* (Oxford: Blackwell).
Maxwell, Nicholas (1998), *The Comprehensibility of the Universe* (Oxford: OUP).
Maxwell, Nicholas (2001), *The Human World in the Physical Universe* (Rowman and Littlefield).

COMMENTS ON HODGSON

J.J.C. Smart

David Hodgson's paper is not a simple one on which to comment. His knowledge of the literature is vast and sophisticated, and in defending the libertarian position he shows that he is fully aware of the usual objections to forms of it. In particular he is fully aware of the theory that free will is compatible with determinism, or perhaps determinism about the brain with only a little bit of pure chance thrown in, which can give a pragmatic justification for many of our usual moral and legal conventions about responsibility and blame and punishment.

Hodgson does not attempt to give a knock down argument against compatibilists but is concerned to give a novel and ingenious form of it that is nevertheless consonant with what 'the plain person' tends to think. Whether Hodgson's theory really is the plain person's is another matter, since most plain persons lack the theoretical sophistication required. I would contend that compatibilism can give the plain person and indeed the legal profession most of what he or it wants from a theory of free will, but not all because the plain person wants an impossibility, that we should be determined by our beliefs, desires, and our characters and yet not be determined. Hodgson argues that we can indeed have it both ways. Indeed he allows for the fact that we are good at predicting one another's behaviour, and as David Hume put it 'a prisoner — discovers the impossibility of his escape as much from the obduracy of the jailer as the walls and bars with which he is surrounded' (Hume, *Inquiry Concerning Human Understanding*, Section VIII).

It might at first appear that there *is* a knock down argument against the libertarian position. We first define determinism and then define pure chance as the negation of determinism. (Smart, 1961). Then logic seems to leave no room for libertarian free will. Of course the libertarian has an easy reply, namely that the negation of determinism is not pure chance but is the disjunction of pure chance and libertarian free will (Campbell, 1963). Of course this obliges the person who takes this line to give definition or at any rate elucidations of the notions not only of determinism but also that of acting by libertarian free will and also of pure chance. A favourite definition of determinism was that given by Laplace and is in terms of predictability: The universe is deterministic if a demon with a sufficiently powerful intelligence and which knew the laws of nature and the whole state of the universe at time t_1 could calculate the state of the universe at any later (or indeed earlier) time t_2. (In the context of the free will debate we need consider only predictions not retrodictions.) We can also use a similar definition in the context of limited idealized systems rather than of the whole universe. Thus in the case of the free will dispute we might consider the brain and all its sensory stimuli as an isolated system. If the powerful intelligence was supposed to think inside a formalised language the definition is a syntactical one. To avoid certain technical objections it is better to use a model theoretic (semantical) definition (Montague, 1974; also Earman, 1986). One of the various advantages of the model theoretic definition is that there are chaotic systems which we would want to call 'deterministic' and which fall under the model theoretic definition but do not admit of predictability because the time needed to do the deduction increases faster than the number of steps in the deduction and so the calculation never terminates. So the model theoretic approach does not provide a way of escape for those who dislike the thought of the universe being deterministic. Hodgson agrees that chaos theory does not help the libertarian.

Hodgson defines determinism with the aid of the concept of causation. I myself try to avoid this because of this concept's imprecision and contextual nature. However for present purposes Hodgson and I do not need to quibble over the exact notion of determinism. We could well agree that determinism if not the contradictory of pure chance is at least a contrary. It is necessary to distinguish the notion of pure chance from our ordinary notion of chance. Thus Aristotle elucidates chance in effect as the intersection of two apparently unrelated causal chains (*Physics* 196b–197b). A man walking home from the pub is hit on the head by a loose tile falling from a roof. If he had not stopped on his way to show someone the way to the church he would have escaped injury, as he would have if the gust of wind that loosened the tile had occurred a few seconds sooner. This is quite compatible with determinism. How should we define the pure chance that is incompatible with determinism? For the reasons that I have given above, I cannot in a discussion with a libertarian such as Hodgson define pure chance simply as the negation of determinism. If we had a clear notion of libertarian free will we could treat 'acting from pure chance' as the negation of the disjunction of 'acting deterministically' and 'acting by libertarian free will'. The trouble is that the question at issue is whether we can make sense of the notion of libertarian free will.

It might be thought, as C.A.Campbell (1963 mentioned above) did, that we could get the notion through introspection at the moment of moral choice. Campbell thought that what he called 'contra-causal freedom' occurred only when one's sense of duty opposes one's strongest desire. This Kantian notion is not of a desire (in Kantian terms it is 'will' not desire'). This is psychologically implausible. Sense of duty is inculcated in us by parents, nursemaids, teachers and so on, not to mention sergeant majors. It seems to be naturalistically explicable. In the light of Wittgenstein and other philosophers of language it is very doubtful whether we can get meanings by introspection. When I introspect I find myself saying 'I can do this and I can do that'. The 'can' here seems to me like that in 'If I drop this china plate it can break but might not.' It all depends on the precise initial conditions, for example its angular velocity about a diameter as I let go. On the other hand if I drop an aluminium plate it cannot: break: That is, within the likely range of initial conditions it will not break. The sense of 'can' here is obviously quite compatible with determinism. Of course Campbell might disagree on the philosophy of language, and once this was thrashed out the dispute might merely be shifted to another topic. (And so the dialogue might go on back and forth.) However there would have to be trade off about plausibilities and one or other of the theories might be judged to suffer from epicyclic degeneration or from antecedent judgments of initial background assumptions, for example of the plausibility or otherwise of naturalism. There are never (or hardly ever) knockdown arguments in philosophy (Smart, 1993).

Perhaps in this respect Hodgson is nearer to me than to Campbell. He does not seek apodeictic proof. He does not rely so much on introspection but proposes a bold extension of the notion of laws of physics that he hopes will allow for a libertarian interpretation of the free will 'can'. He takes much account of scientific method though he modifies or extends it by an ingenious extrapolation of the notion of a law of nature. He also makes use of quantum mechanics in two ways. One of these is to use quantum mechanical indeterminism to leave a place for libertarian free will. The other is to use non-locality to allow for the instantaneous coordination between different parts of the brain in the perception of gestalten. I think that we can put the second of these aside in that the comparatively slow movement of signals from neuron to neuron is compatible with perception within a single specious present and not (I think) contradicted by the experiments of Libet *et al.* Or consider the case of a top class batsman in cricket facing an extremely fast bowler. I have read somewhere that he thinks that he is following the ball right on to the bat, allowing for late swing as he plays his shot, whereas in fact he predicts the trajectory of the ball from the way the bowler holds rhe ball and the exact nature of his action. Whether or not this is a correct account of how top class batsmen play an extremely fast ball, the example suggests that it is not obvious that there is a need for non-locality. Of course I do not deny the existence of non-locality in quantum mechanics but I question whether there is a need for the concept in neuroscience.

The more contentious, innovative and ingenious matter is Hodgson's extension of the notion of a law of nature. I wonder whether the notion of law of nature is essential to physics or whether it belongs simply to talk about physics. It seems to me that Newton's *Principia* could have been written equally cogently without the words 'law', 'scholium', 'corollary', and so on. They are not part of the argument but are devices for simplifying the prose and for helping the reader to follow the structure of the argument. Whether this is so or not there seems to be no doubt that Hodgson's proposed extension of the concept of 'law' is vital to his philosophy of free will. As we usually think of them, the laws of nature express regularities. Some philosophers think that they do more than this, such as express natural necessities or relations between universals but there is a general consensus that they at least express regularities. Hodgson proposes that besides the regularity laws, which he calls 'C-laws' there are G-laws and E-laws. C-laws constrain outcomes. G-laws guide outcomes. E-laws 'empower or enable certain emergent systems to direct or select outcomes'. G-laws guide E-systems by providing non–conclusive reasons whereby they 'direct or select outcomes' (Hodgson, 2001, which is a slightly fuller account of his classification of laws than is given in 'the present rather compressed paper'.)

From page 10 above it appears that G-laws have the nature of imperatives or at any rate are on the 'ought' side of the 'is'–'ought' distinction. Hodgson claims that the introduction of G-laws does not bring in the supernatural. I think that this is merely a verbal point. I would suggest that to bring in so-called laws that are in effect in the imperative mood is such a departure from a really physicalist metaphysics that it could deserve the appellation 'supernaturalist'. At any rate it is a partial retreat to an something like an earlier use of 'law of nature' which may derive from Roman jurisprudence and before that the Stoics (Ruby, 1986). Perhaps Hodgson could say 'none the worse for that'. However since the scientific revolution the notion has shed its association with the legal *lex*. Indeed Hodgson has said that in his extension of the notion of 'law of nature' to include G-laws he has indeed been inspired by jurisprudence, drawing attention to distinctions made by the jurist Wesley Hohfeld (Hodgson, 2001, p. 342). C-laws are like laws that impose duties, G-laws are like those that give liberties, and E-laws are like laws that empower a judge to use discretion. Of course the likenesses need to be taken with a grain of salt as Hodgson of course does. Thus it makes no sense to talk of a planet disobeying the laws of mechanics. Mercury seemed to deviate from Newton's laws but this showed that Newton's laws were not quite right and that general relativity was right and nearer the truth. (Here I am equivocating, I hope harmlessly, between 'law' and 'statement of law'.)

The E-laws allow for the emergence of totally novel properties, not in any way reducible to more basic laws and the configurations to which these apply much as the properties of a radio are explicable by physics plus wiring diagrams. Hodgson's sense of 'emergence' is a very strong one that I have discussed elsewhere(Smart 1981a). Hodgson proposes that by virtue of E-laws certain complexes will possess consciousness. They may also possess libertarian free will. The G-laws provide mere guidance and do not determine outcomes. Hodgson holds that the emergence of consciousness is an important consequence of the E-laws. This is because Hodgson's theory of choice involves reference to the perception of gestalten.

As I have indicated above it is not clear that there is a problem about perception of gestalten that requires such a drastic extension of current physics. I would urge the same about consciousness. It may well be that consciousness in the full sense is just awareness of awareness, coming to believe by inner sense about the brain processes that are the comings to believe about the external world (Smart, 2004, and Armstrong in Armstrong and Malcolm, 1962). We approximate to mere awareness when we go on to 'automatic pilot' as Armstrong has put it. Inner sense is perception of the brain by itself. Armstrong has described it as analogous to proprioception. The second order awareness would have evolutionary value because of its monitoring of first order awareness. No doubt there can be awareness of awareness, awareness of awareness of awareness, a step or two up, but at the top there will be awareness without awareness of it. This may explain our illusion of the ineffability of consciousness. Compare Ryle on the systematic elusiveness of 'I' (Ryle, 1949, pp.195–8). Probably this account of conscious- ness needs improving but it does not seem to me to be plausible that we will need anything so drastic as Hodgson's introduction of G-laws and E-laws. These laws relate specifically to conscious beings and I would suggest that after we have cured ourselves of thinking of the earth as the centre of the universe and of anthropocentrism we should be suspicious of what one may call 'psychocentrism'. Consciousness might be rather small beer in the cosmic scheme of things.

Hodgson suggests that if consciousness was not necessary for perception of gestalten and for free choice then it would confer no selective advantage and indeed that if one were confronted by a crisis, for example the approach of a tiger, natural selection would not have made us waste our mental power on consciousness, whereas the opposite is the case: if a man eating tiger approaches a man he has heightened consciousness. I can agree about the heightened consciousness but draw a different conclusion: the more critical the situation the more important it may be to monitor one's awareness.

At one point Hodgson elucidates libertarian free will as being guided by reasons as opposed to causes. This puzzles me because in neither of two possible senses of 'reason' in this context is there need to deny compatibilism. In one sense of 'reason' reasons *are* causes (Davidson, 1980). If I say 'The reason for Jones coming home a little late was his desire to consult a colleague' the word 'reason' is meant to refer to a cause, namely the desire. On the other hand if Jones's wife asks for his reason she may be asking for a justification and not a cause. She might say 'That could have waited until tomorrow: I was in a hurry for us to go to the hospital before the end of visiting hours'. There seems to be no reason here to invoke libertarian choice.

I do indeed find great difficulty in grasping the libertarian notion of free will. This should be no surprise to those of us who think that the notion is incoherent. Let me consider another way of defining it. Suppose that we are willing to define 'chance' by reference to the sense in which it (or ø or probability) occurs in quantum mechanics so that the testable theory would give us some purchase on it. Then libertarian free will could be defined as neither determinism nor pure chance However those of us who are comfortable with compatibilism will want a more positive characterisation of libertarian free will.

Indeed I suggest that we should be comfortable not only with compatibilism but even with a weak form of fatalism that is consistent with indeterminism. In the four-dimensional world of relativity the future is as real as the past. There it is tenseless ahead of us (us now) in Minkowski space (Smart, 1981b). I would argue that it is as real as the past anyway. This is not to accept the silly form of fatalism that holds that the future does not depend on what we do. Of course it does. The soldier was killed because he put his head above the trench. If he had not the future would have contained a live soldier, not a dead one. It does matter what we do. Notions of responsibility, punishment and reward can still be appropriate in society. Jones resists the temptation to commit burglary because he knows why Smith ended up in prison. There need not be anything inhumane about compatibilisn or even weak fatalism. Indeed compatibilism may be more consonant with humaneness than with retributive theories of punishment because it at least suggests that we should inflict minimum punishments consistent with deterring others and protecting the public I am not of course suggesting that retributionists are never humane. Still this is another matter. Here we are concerned not with morality but with truth.

The attraction of Hodgson's theory seems to lie in its emotional appeal and also on a reliance on phenomenology which I distrust. The trade off for its metaphysical complications and, despite Hodgson's ingenuity, its apparent obscurity, is too hard won. Of course to say 'I don't understand', looking up at the ceiling with eyebrows raised in the neo-Wittgensteinian manner (whereupon the other person is supposed to have lost the argument because he is supposed to have said something meaningless), is too dangerous a matter. The only time I saw Bertrand Russell read a paper was when in the discussion one brash young philosopher tried this ploy, whereupon Russell said ' I'm not responsible for your intellectual deficiencies, young man'. I hope that Hodgson will not think me too like this young man.

References

Armstrong, D.M. and Malcolm, N. (1962), *Consciousness and Causality* (London: Routledge).
Campbell, C.A. (1951), 'Is "freewill" a pseudo-problem?' *Mind* **60**, pp. 291–306.
Campbell, C.A. (1963), 'Professor Smart on "Freewill, praise and blame": A reply', *Mind*, **72**, pp. 44–65.
Davidson, D. (1980), *Actions, Reasons and Causes* (Oxford Clarendon Press).
Earman, J. (1986), *A Primer on Determinism* (Dordrecht: Kluwer).
Hodgson, D. (2001), 'Constraint, empowerment and guidance: A conjectural classification of laws of nature', *Philosophy* **76**, pp. 341–70.
Montague, R. (1974), *Formal Philosophy* (New Haven and London: Yale University Press).
Ruby, J.E. (1986), 'The origins of scientific "law"', *Journal of the History of Ideas*, **47**, pp. 341–59).
Ryle, G. (1949), *The Concept of Mind* (London: Hutchinson).
Smart, J.J.C. (1961), 'Freewill, praise and blame', *Mind* **70**, pp. 291–306.
Smart, J.J.C. (1981a), 'Physicalism and emergence', *Neuroscience,* **6,** pp. 141–50. Reprinted in Smart (1987).
Smart, J.J.C. (1981b), 'The reality of the future', *Philosophia*, **10**, pp. 141–50. Reprinted in Smart 1987.
Smart, J.J.C. (1987), *Essays Metaphysical and Moral* (Oxford: Blackwell).
Smart, J.J.C. (1993), 'Why philosophers disagree', in *Reconstructing Philosophy: New Essays on Metaphilosophy*, ed. Jocelyne Couture and Kai Nielsen (Calgary, Alberta: University of Calgary Press), pp.67–82. Also in *Canadian Journal of Philosophy*, Supplementary Volume **19.**
Smart, J.J.C. (2004), 'Consciousness and awareness', *Journal of Consciousness Studies*, **11** (2), pp. 41–50.

THE VIEW FROM WITHIN

Sean A. Spence

David Hodgson has provided a phenomenological account of what it is like to be a conscious agent, aware of making choices in the world. From this perspective, describing the appearance of things, there is little in his essay with which to disagree. Most of us have the recurring experience that we initiate our actions; sometimes we weigh up the alternatives, sometimes we seem to follow our habits and proclivities. We become aware of the consequences of the things that we have done and, ultimately, within a society of similar beings, we are held accountable for our actions (unless, of course, there is compelling evidence of our psychopathology).

So, there is little here that appears contentious; indeed, societies have worked along similar lines for millennia. There would seem to be no need to rock the boat.

But does phenomenology provide a sufficient account for all situations? Consider the phenomenology of my observing the sun. From this subject's perspective it appears that the sun rotates around the earth; at least it seems eminently reasonable to state that the sun 'rises' in the east and 'sets' in the west. Indeed, many human beings have lived and died believing that this is the case, with the earth at the centre of things. From a phenomenological perspective this all seems rather obvious. Yet, as our knowledge of the nature of things expands it causes us to question many of our natural assumptions. We come to learn that the earth is not the centre of the universe and the sun does not rotate around us. From an everyday perspective this item of knowledge need not impact upon us too greatly although much of the time, at a level unseen to us, such knowledge informs some of the technologies we use.

So, phenomenology provides a reasonable account of the surface of things but there might be levels of knowledge, appropriate to other, technical circumstances, against which phenomenology would appear rather imprecise. In Hodgson's account we read a defence of free will, at the level of conscious experience, which might be fine for day-to-day living; he calls it 'a plain person's free will'. But is it sufficient?

As I have stated, one could spend much of one's time, in non-specialised or non-reflective situations completely within the phenomenology that Hodgson describes. Indeed, at intervals in his essay, he anticipates critique arising only from specialised authors (philosophers and cognitive scientists). However, critique of Hodgson's position need not be solely contemporary in origin; there are many accounts from antiquity onward suggesting that contemplatives have come to question whether the conscious mind is the origin of human conduct. Often this is stated in terms of the conscious mind not knowing the reasons for certain behaviours that emerge, but also there is an acknowledgement that agents may not know what they will do until they see what they have done. Hence, authors have identified the constraints upon our knowledge of our selves and the temporal control of our actions since well before the modern age.

I think the problem arises for Hodgson when he attempts to move from phenomenology to some other level of accounting for voluntary action. There is a problem when an experience is equated with its own causation. I *feel* as if I am choosing, therefore it is my *feeling* of choice which is choosing [imagine if I stated it was my experience of seeing which was the cause of my seeing; the problem might become more obvious]. Hodgson wants to hold on to the moment of choice as somehow being above the causal chain that precedes it. Yes, circumstances may affect our actions, yes genes and environment play their roles, yes there may be individual constraints, but there is nevertheless some special something which sits at the end of the causal chain, equivalent in everyone, which makes the decision, without recourse to either causation or chance, and which is responsible. This special something sounds very much like a soul, yet Hodgson denies that his solution is spiritual.

The problem for Hodgson's account is that it is really a restatement of the basic phenomenology of conscious choice. His critique of alternative views is cursory. While I might point out that recourse to Quantum Mechanics seems a commonplace among writers within the consciousness field, replacing one mystery with another, I shall examine one specific area touched upon by Hodgson: the biology of action at the moment of choice.

In the 1980s Benjamin Libet and colleagues published a series of experiments that used electroencephalography (EEG) to study the brain events preceding subjects' conscious choice of action (Libet *et al.*, 1983). In these experiments subjects chose when to move a finger, the constraint being that they had to keep note of when they made their decision, relative to the movements of a clock. Over many trials of the protocol the experimenters were able to time lock the subjects' EEG signals to their movements. They found predictive trains of electrical activity arising from the motor regions of the brain prior to the act itself. This finding is unremarkable as one would expect there to be a finite period required for the brain to transmit the requisite signals to the periphery during the initiation of a motor act. However, what was more interesting was that when the moment of subjective choice was compared with the ongoing activity leading up to the motor act, it too was found to be preceded by hundreds of milliseconds of brain activity. In other words, coherent brain activity preceded the subjects' conscious awareness of their decision to act 'spontaneously'. Libet's findings have been regarded as controversial and various philosophers have attempted to discount them, but they have been replicated in other laboratories. In his essay, Hodgson attempts to discount them by saying that they relate only to the choice between doing something and doing nothing (as if this were trivial!), but the same effect can be seen when choosing which of two actions to perform.

If we regard the physical constraints acting upon our selves and our brains as real then it should not surprise us that even the prized phenomena of voluntary behaviours exhibit finite delays and processing intervals. Libet and colleagues also went on to show that sensory information reaching the brain requires a certain time (a period of 'neuronal adequacy') for it to access consciousness (Libet, 1993). In other words, there is a finite period of activity required for information to become conscious, and a temporal window during which incoming information may be disturbed (e.g., by electrical stimulation), leading to the brain failing to 'experience' it as a conscious percept. Again, such findings serve to illustrate the biological constraints within which the human organism functions. It is ironic that they also serve to undermine Libet's own account of the conscious free will as much as they do Hodgson's.

Although Libet's work clearly seems to undermine the causal role of conscious cognition in chosen activities, his own solution to this problem was to argue that consciousness has a power of 'veto' over emerging acts. Hence, although the action in question is initiated prior to conscious awareness, consciousness may stop the act if 'it' regards it as inappropriate. Like Hodgson's account this seems eminently reasonable [if inherently dualistic], at a phenomenological level, as we often have the conscious awareness of stopping ourselves from some course of action that we might otherwise be just about to embark upon. Yet there is a problem with Libet's defence of conscious freedom that emerges from the logic of his own preceding work (Spence, 1996). For if there is a finite period of neural activity required for any percept to emerge into consciousness, then is it not the case that this will apply to the feeling of stopping an ongoing course of action? And if the latter is the case, then is the feeling of cessation not itself the late (phenomenological) correlate of a preceding neural event? In other words, if my awareness of my chosen act follows my brain's initiation of that act might not my feeling of stopping an act follow my brain's cessation of it? In either case, although I experience a feeling of volition, the decisive activity has already taken place within my brain.

If we are interested in the moment at which the brain initiates action, then there are other experiments that may inform our thinking. Our group has recently used event-related functional magnetic resonance imaging (efMRI) to study the neural correlates of the moment of freely pressing one of two possible buttons, and the seconds before the action emerges (Hunter *et al.*, 2003). Though our temporal resolution is not as good as that obtained using EEG, we have been able to discern events at the level of 500 milliseconds. We have shown that when subjects are about to press a button specific regions of the prefrontal cortex are activated and that in the second preceding action there is a sequence to the activations seen within the frontal lobes. Activations in prefrontal and premotor areas occur significantly earlier than those in the motor cortex. Indeed, we can even begin to tease apart the correlates of choosing *which* finger to press from those of choosing *when* to press. None of these findings is discernable in the world of phenomenology at the level of persons, but each may bear upon the neurology of what transpires in disease states. One problem for the clinician reading the work of philosophers is their inherent (and perhaps necessary) abstraction from the reality of biology. The man with Parkinson's disease who is unable to initiate an action exemplifies the failure of the will that occurs when brain systems breakdown. The woman who cannot speak when a stroke impacts upon her 'speech' areas exemplifies the reality, the dirty biology of what it is to be a human agent, and all too fragile. If philosophers wish to address the *basis* of the will, rather than its appearances, then I would submit that they would increasingly have to understand neurobiology.

As well as the temporal constraints upon what consciousness can be said to do, there are constraints upon our *degree* of choice. This point is well exemplified in a classic series of experiments by Alan Baddeley. Getting subjects to generate sequences of random responses, at different temporal frequencies, and from differing set sizes of exemplars, Baddeley demonstrated that the ability to generate novel responses is constrained, as if it were a module of finite, limited capacity (Baddeley, 1966). Hence, as subjects responded at increasing frequencies, their responses became more stereotypic ('redundant' in terms of their information content) and, similarly, when the set of possible response exemplars increased (e.g., from numbers 1–4, to numbers 1–32) subjects took longer to respond. Hence, the performance of the subject, generating responses, is constrained by temporal (time to respond) and capacity (range of response alternatives) factors, exhibiting decrements in predictable ways. There are constraints upon human action and some of them may be shown to behave in lawful ways.

Again, these findings have been replicated and we ourselves have elicited them in healthy subjects and also shown how people with certain neuropsychiatric disorders have further constrained patterns of responding (Spence *et al.*, 2002). The choice a subject makes is not independent of their brain function. It behaves as if it is dependent upon it (see figure 1, in which the degree of randomness of response sequence subjects exhibit is correlated with activation in their prefrontal regions). This regularity in human behaviour also forms the basis of a large neuropsychological literature demonstrating that patients with lesions in specific areas of their brains may be unable to initiate chosen actions or may repeat the choices they make (perseverate), even when the context has changed and their choices have become inappropriate.

Finally, the notion that human choice is independent of genes as well as brain (as proposed by Hodgson) would seem to be refuted by a recent finding from Daniel Weinberger's group (Egan *et al.*, 2001). Taking account of individual

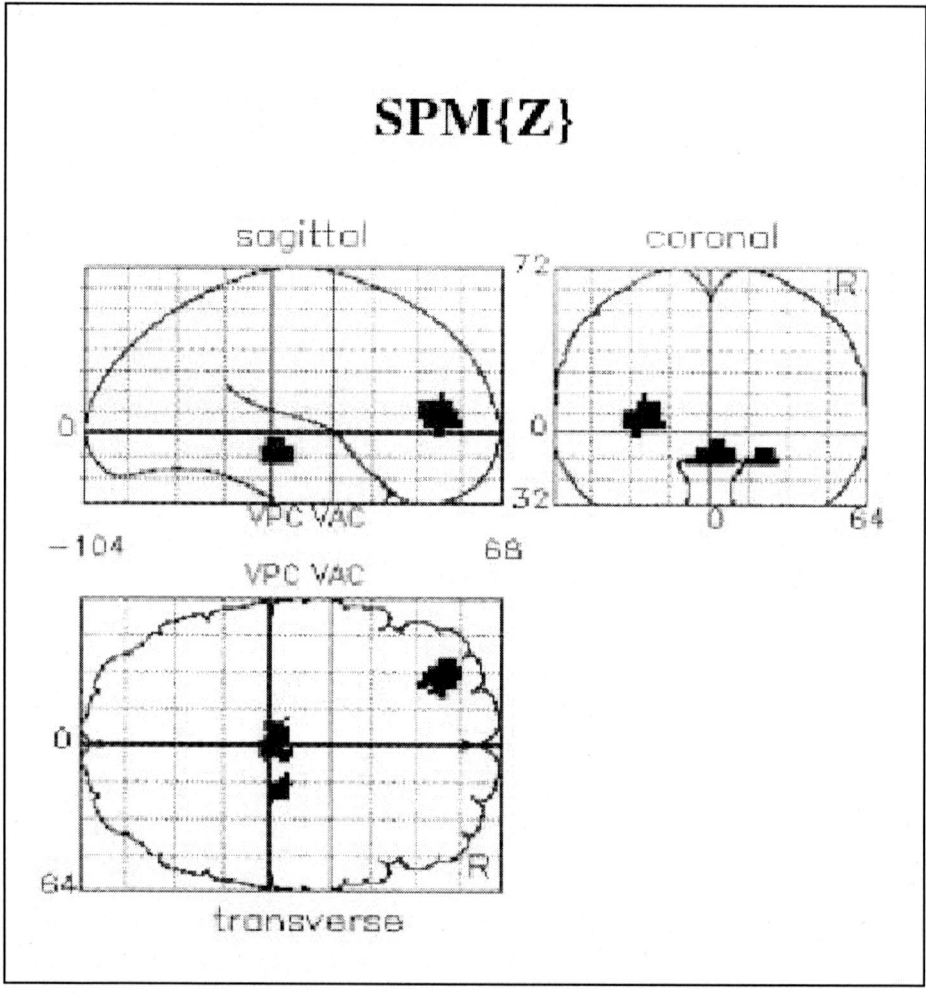

Figure 1. A brain map showing the areas of the brain where activation is positively correlated with degree of randomness of responding by a group of 6 healthy men performing a joystick task. While performing the task at a fixed rate of movement (once every 3 seconds), the subjects had to move a joystick, which allowed four possible directions of movement. Subjects were instructed to make the sequence of their movements as random as possible. Data extracted from Spence et al (1998). The brain is viewed from the right side ('sagittal'), behind ('coronal') and above ('transverse'). With increasing randomness of response sequence there is greater activity in left prefrontal cortex and central subcortical areas (in and inferior to the thalamus)(statistical parametric maps, thresholded at P<0.001, uncorrected).

subjects' genotypes for a polymorphism of a gene involved in the metabolism of dopamine (a transmitter implicated in the generation of novelty by the prefrontal cortex) they showed that on a neuropsychological test, requiring the subject to find solutions to a problem, 4 % of the variance in perseveration, or repetitiveness, of the subjects' responses could be explained by the genotype they possessed. Hence, if one gene can impact upon voluntary behaviour to this extent it is conceivable that others may also play a part in determining what we choose to do. If the degree of flexibility of response that we can make as individuals in a given context is partially attributable to our genes, then our choosing is not equivalent, and we are not as free as each other *in that context*.

I am sympathetic to the strand of Hodgson's proposal that wishes to retain the role of consciousness in volition and the importance of responsibility in human affairs. However, such language is best deployed at the level of the person, and it is my reading of the available evidence that while consciousness itself is necessary for meaningful, purposeful human action, its role may be rather to acquaint us with what has just occurred, and thereby to influence (through feedback mechanisms) what is next to be done (Spence, 1996).

We are responsible for our actions, as persons, but our consciousness of our actions is not synonymous with their causation.

References

Baddeley, A.D. (1966), 'The capacity for generating information by randomness', *Q J Exp Psychol*, **18**, pp. 119–29.

Egan, M.F., Goldberg, T.E., Kolachana, B.S., Callicott, J.H., Mazzanti, C.M., Straub, R.E., Goldman, D. and Weinberger, D.R. (2001), 'Effect of COMT Val 108/158 Met genotype on frontal lobe function and risk for schizophrenia', *PNAS*, **98**, pp. 6917–22.

Hunter, M.D., Farrow, T.F.D., Papadakis, N.G., Wilkinson, I.D., Woodruff, P.W.R. and Spence, S.A. (2003), 'Approaching an ecologically valid functional anatomy of spontaneous "willed" action', *NeuroImage*, **20**, pp. 1264–9.

Libet, B. (1993), 'The neural time factor in conscious and unconscious events', in *Experimental and Theoretical Studies of Consciousness*, Ciba Foundation Symposium 174 (Chichester: Wiley), pp. 123–46.

Libet, B., Gleason, C.A., Wright, E.W. and Pearl, D.K. (1983), 'Time of conscious intention to act in relation to onset of cerebral activity', *Brain*, **106**, pp. 623–42.

Spence, S.A. (1996), 'Free will in the light of neuropsychiatry', *Phil Psychiatry Psychol*, **3**, pp. 75–90.

Spence, S.A., Hunter, M.D. and Harpin, G. (2003), 'Neuroscience and the will', *Curr Opin Psychiatry*, **15**, pp. 519–26.

Spence, S.A., Hirsch, S.R., Brooks, D.J. and Grasby, P.M. (1998), 'Prefrontal activity in people with schizophrenia and control subjects: Evidence from positron emission tomography for remission of "hypofrontality" with remission from acute schizophrenia', *Br J Psychiatry*, **172**, pp. 316–23.

COMMENTARY ON HODGSON

Henry Stapp

Hodgson aims to present a scientifically and philosophically respectable defense of the claim 'that free will exists and is inconsistent with determinism.' His argument depends upon an important claim made and defended in Hodgson (2002). That claim is that nature has two different kinds of processes: quantitative processes and qualitative processes. Quantitative processes are based on *mathematical descriptions*, and can be general. They can be deterministic and/or random, but can merely *constrain*: they may leave certain options open. Qualitative processes occur only under special conditions, and allow agents/subjects to grasp or feel whole gestalts, and make judgments that are influenced by these feelings. These judgments can influence *selections* that can choose between options left open by the quantitative process.

In the target article Hodgson elaborates upon his earlier argument by stating and defending nine propositions. The linchpin is Proposition 5, which asserts that 'the subject makes an effective non-random selection between the available alternatives, based on these non-conclusive reasons, albeit not determined by rules or laws of nature.'

Hodgson's arguments supporting Proposition 5 are, as he himself admits, 'difficult.' For example, he gives an argument based on evolution to support his contention that there is in the selection process an element 'that is not accounted for by strict rules of any kind.' He says 'If choices were in fact determined by algorithms, such as evolution-selected computation-like procedures, which *as algorithms* need no help from conscious judgment, and could indeed be hindered by conscious interference, there could be no plausible explanation of why evolution selected in favour of brains that, at considerable expense in terms of complexity and energy-use, support conscious processes.' However, this argument does not justify, or even support, the conclusion that the selection processes cannot be 'accounted for by strict rules of any kind.' What it is difficult to understand is how such a selection process could produce pertinent determinate actions or beliefs without any rules. What the argument certainly does buttress is the idea that the selection process needs to give real causal efficacy to our thoughts, ideas, and feelings *themselves*, in order for these *qualitative* feature of reality to have a non-redundant functional role in the unfolding of the world, and hence a reason to exist and to evolve. But that does not mean that this functional role of consciousness is achieved without *rules of any kind.*

Hodgson's thesis is incompatible with the truth of classical physics, in which all physical activity is fixed by local mechanical laws from initial physical conditions. Thus Hodgson appeals to quantum mechanics (QM). However, he creates unnecessary difficulties by asserting both that that the selection process is 'inconsistent with determinism' and is 'nonrandom,' and that 'according to QM, any indeterminism is mere randomness.' It is not true that QM says that 'any indeterminism is mere randomness.' If it did, then Hodgson's claim that the selection process is both inconsistent with determinism and non-random would mean that the selection process would not be consistent with QM, and his appeal to QM would fail to achieve its objective. But, in fact, contemporary orthodox quantum mechanics explicitly introduces a selection process that is neither fixed by any known deterministic rule nor subject to any known statistical rule, but which has, by virtue of the known (i.e., postulated) deterministic and statistical laws, specified impacts on the course of physical events.

Orthodox QM has *three* processes: the locally deterministic Schroedinger equation, the random 'choice on the part of nature,' and the process called Process **1** by von Neumann. This process **1** is absolutely essential, and it involves an element of 'choice.' It constitutes the major departure of QM from classical mechanics, *because it brings actions selected and performed by human agents directly into the fundamental structure of the theory.* The causal roots of these *choices* are not specified by the theory. Nor are there any statistical constraints on these choices. They are, explicitly, 'Free Choices,' not in the strong sense that the theory dogmatically asserts that they have no causal roots at all, but in the weak sense that contemporary orthodox QM treats them as *free parameters,* at the level of practical application of the theory, and evades speculation pertaining to the causal roots of these choices.

Orthodox Copenhagen QM is formulated in a realistic and practical way. It is structured around the activities of human agents, who are considered able to freely elect to probe a system of interest in any one of many possible ways. Bohr emphasized the freedom of the experimenters in passages such as:

> The freedom of experimentation, presupposed in classical physics, is of course retained and corresponds to the free choice of experimental arrangement for which the mathematical structure of the quantum mechanical formalism offers the appropriate latitude (Bohr, 1958, p. 73).

The fact that the causal roots of these 'free choices' *are not specified by contemporary QM* stems from the fact that in the original Copenhagen formulation of quantum theory the human experimenter is considered to stand outside the system to which the quantum laws are applied. Those quantum laws are the only precise laws of nature recognized by that theory. Thus, according to the Copenhagen philosophy, *there are no presently known laws that govern the choices* made by the agent about how he or she will act upon the quantum system that he or she is probing.

The introduction of choices made by participating agents directly into the dynamics constitutes a profound change in the principles of physics, as understood and applied in QM as contrasted to classical mechanics. This switch is greatly celebrated and much discussed, and is epitomized in Niels Bohr's dictum that ' in the great drama of existence we ourselves are both actors and spectators.' (Bohr, 1963, p. 15; 1958, p. 81) The emphasis here is on 'actors': in classical physics the human agents were treated essentially as spectators. But orthodox Copenhagen QM is formulated only within the context of agents acting on systems and observing what happens. The choices made by the agents as to how they will act play an essential role in the extraction from the theory of predictions pertaining to the outcomes of observations, *and these 'free choices' can strongly influence the course of physical events in the observed system.*

These 'free choices' are normally experienced as being determined by a thought or idea, such as a desire to test some theory, or to determine some parameter. There is no basis in contemporary physics to deny the strong intuition that our thoughts, ideas, and feelings do affect our choices of how to act, while being themselves not determined solely by the physically described aspects of nature.

The second part of the tripartite quantum process is 'causal'. It is specified by the Schroedinger equation of motion, and is locally and globally deterministic. Von Neumann calls this causal component Process **2**.

The third process in contemporary QM is ruled by 'chance'. Dirac called this process a 'choice on the part of nature.' It picks out, in way governed only by a statistical rule, a definite outcome of the probing action selected by Process **1**.

In orthodox Copenhagen QM the agent is taken to include not only his own physical body and stream of conscious experiences, but also his measuring devices. His actions and resulting observations — as represented within his stream of consciousness — are described in a language that allows him to communicate to colleagues what he has done and what he has learned.

The agent acts intentionally upon the system being probed in order to elicit an experiential feedback that can be recognized. The agent's choice of action specifies a reduction of the state of the system being examined into two subsystems, one corresponding to the occurrence of the recognizable positive feedback, the other corresponding to the non-occurrence of that response. This theoretical structure allows the actions and feedbacks, described in terms of experiences residing in the stream of consciousness of the agent, to become correlated to mathematically/physically described properties of the system being examined.

This connection between physical description and conscious experience is the basis of science. Copenhagen quantum theory brings into science the very activity *of doing science*, and replaces certain ontological features of classical physical that turn out to be unknowable in principle by the knowable, communicable, and partly controllable conscious experiences that constitute the empirical foundation of scientific practice.

This Copenhagen formulation is pragmatically useful. But it is not suitable for analysing the connection between the experiences of an agent and his physical brain. That is because the brain and body of the agent are, in the Copenhagen scheme, not parts of the physically described system. However, John von Neumann (1932/1955) formulated QM in a way that allows (the quantum counterparts of) all of the particles in the universe to be included in the physically described part of the theory, with only the streams of consciousness of agents being described in terms of the way we experience objects, intentions, and feelings.

In this von Neumann form of QM the brain of the agent becomes the system being probed by the experientially described agent. The physically described system *is treated* as an objectively existing system, even though it effectively represents knowledge, information, and tendencies for experiential mind-brain events to occur. Each event E in a stream of consciousness is an experiential event that occurs in conjunction with a physical event in the brain of the experiencing agent. This physical event is specified by a definite mathematical structure $P(E)$ acting on the brain of the agent. This action actualizes the neural correlates of the conscious experience E.

This connection between conscious experiences and their neural correlates is a key part of the theory, and it ties neatly into neuroscience, which is now seriously endeavouring to map out the connection between human experiences and their neural correlates.

The action of consciousness upon brain events can have important consequences not only for individual events but also for statistical average values. Thus our conscious thoughts, although themselves undetermined by the presently known laws of physics, can have important effects on what the brain does. This reverses the relationship that held in classical physics, where conscious experiences were imagined to be completely determine by the brain, but could play no irreplaceable role in what the brain does, because all brain activity is determined by the initial physical conditions of the universe together with local mechanical laws that never acknowledge the existence of conscious experiences.

Persons accustomed to thinking about physics in *classical* terms may consider far-fetched the idea of introducing experiential qualities into the basic equations of brain dynamics. If, following Isaac Newton, one considers the world to be made of 'solid, massy, hard, impenetrable, movable particles' (Newton, 1721) that move in accordance with immutable deterministic laws that fix the entire course of history from initial conditions, then the idea that experiential qualities enter in a non-redundant and non-eliminable way into the flow of physical events might seem to be absurd. But quantum phenomena show the concepts of classical physics to be inconsistent with the observed behaviour of the world, and the new theory, Copenhagen QM, replaces that classical materialist conception of the physical world by an essentially 'idea-like' structure. The physical state represents 'our knowledge,' rather than material substance, and is used to compute predictions about what we will find out if we probe nature in various alternative possible ways. Von Neumann's generalization of the Copenhagen version of QM gives a theory of the mind-brain that explicitly involves both idea-like and matter-like features. In view of this un-sought — and initially stoutly resisted — entry of idea-like qualities into the basic structure of physics it is no longer irrational to believe that idea-like qualities may play an essential role in brain dynamics. Of course, a priori reasonableness is not enough in science: a scientific theory must deliver the goods. Some consequences of pursuing this line in psychology and neuroscience are described in Stapp (2001; 2003) and Schwartz (Schwartz & Begley, 2002; Schwartz *et al.*, 2004; 2005).

Hodgson's final aim is to provide a scientifically respectable and rational theory of personal responsibility. He argues that, to rescue the concept of personal responsibility, the choices must be free, in the strong sense of being 'inconsistent with determinism' and 'not accounted for by strict rules of any kind.' '…the subject makes an effective non-random selection between the available alternatives, based on these non-conclusive reasons, albeit not determined by strict rules or laws of nature.'

The first main point of this commentary is that these conditions on the choices made by human agents are completely in line with contemporary basic physical theory. They conflict with features of classical physics that have *not been retained* in contemporary physical theory. Quantum theory brings the human observer into the causal structure in an important way, while not specifying, as yet, any rules that fix the observer's causally efficacious choices about how to act.

The absence of these rules in contemporary physical theory does not mean that definite experiences occur without rules of any kind. Hodgson's insistence that the qualitative process be both non-deterministic and non-random was meant to rescue the concept of personal responsibility from the argument that a person cannot be held responsible for any action that was already pre-determined before he or she was born, or was determined by random choices beyond his or her control. However, personal responsibility is rooted not in the *ultimate* causes of an agent's actions but in the *immediate* causes of those actions. The personal responsibility of a human being arises from his or her nature as a human being: as an agent that is able to grasp and be moved by the meaning of the complex informational structures that have been instantiated in his or her brain by the sequence of mind-brain events whose mental sides constitute his or her stream of consciousness. It arises from his or her character as the thinking, reflecting, selecting, and physically efficacious agent that deep intuition proclaims him or her to be, as contrasted to the essentially mindless automaton ruled by local mechanical process that nineteenth century philosophers, and even some twentieth century philosophers, mistakenly claimed him or her to be. The whole idea of 'determinism,' as applied to human beings, is reshaped in the passage from classical physics to quantum physics, because in the latter case all of the depth of holistic graspings of meanings and values can enter in irreplaceable and non-mechanical ways into the determination of an action.

In view of these considerations I believe that Hodgson's arguments can be strengthened by (1) emphasizing how his first thesis — that our conscious choices need not be completely determined by algorithmic physical processes, and yet can strongly influence our physical actions — is not contrary to physics but is in fact exemplified by contemporary physical theory, and (2) dropping the condition that our selections are not 'accounted for by strict rules of any kind.' Rules that give full weight to the causal efficacy of a person's consciously constructed value system and to the consequence of the processes of plausible reasoning that occur both consciously and unconsciously in the dynamics of that person's mind-brain do not, I believe, contravene the principle of personal responsibility.

Acknowledgements

This article has benefited from comments on earlier drafts by David Hodgson, Aaron Sloman, Kathryn Laskey, Stan Klein and Ken Augustyn.

References

Bohr, N. (1958), *Atomic Physics and Human Knowledge* (New York: Wiley).
Bohr, N. (1963), Essays 1958/1962 on *Atomic Physics and Human* Knowledge (New York: Wiley).
Newton, I. (1721), *Opticks*. 3rd ed. London: Printed for William and John Innys. p. 375/6.
Schwartz, J. and Begley, S. (2002), *The Mind and the Brain* (Harper Collins, New York).

Schwartz, J.M., Stapp, H.P. and Beauregard, M. (2004), 'The volitional influence of the mind on the brain, with special reference to emotional self-regulation', in *Consciousness, Emotional Self-Regulation and the Brain*, ACR 54 (Amsterdam/Philadlphia: John Benjamins).

Schwartz, J.M., Stapp, H.P. and Beauregard, M. (2005), 'Quantum theory in neuroscience and psychology: A neurophysical model of mind/brain interaction', *Phil. Trans. Roy. Soc. (Biol. Sect.)*. In press.

Stapp, H. (2001), 'Quantum theory and the role of mind in nature', *Found. of Phys.* 11, pp. 1465–99.

Stapp, H. (2003), 'Neuroscience, atomic physics, and the human person' in *Mind, Matter, and Quantum Mechanics*, 2nd Ed. (Berlin & New York: Springer). Ch 12.

Von Neumann, J. (1955/1932), *Mathematical Foundations of Quantum Mechanics*, trans. Robert T. Beyer from the 1932 German original (Princeton: Princeton University Press) Ch VI.

ADD YOUR VOICE TO THE DEBATE

Readers are invited to add their own commentary on David Hodgson's paper, or to respond to any of the printed commentaries, by posting a message to the moderated discussion forum **jcs-online**.

MEMBERSHIP OF THE FORUM IS FREE

To sign on, post a blank email to:

jcs-online-subscribe@yahoogroups.com

David Hodgson

Response To Commentators

I am very grateful to the commentators for their consideration of my target article. I found their comments thought-provoking and challenging, but I am not persuaded that any substantial departure is required from the views I expressed in the article. I will respond to each comment in turn, and then I will briefly review how my nine propositions have fared.

A.G. Cairns-Smith

The first commentator, Graham Cairns-Smith, seems sympathetic to my position, and even allows that it is possible; though he himself leans towards a 'somewhat weaker' version.

He agrees with me that feelings contribute to our behaviour, but suggests that feelings might be part of a 'piece of clockwork', driving each other (and presumably contributing to our actions) like cogwheels. This is a possibility I acknowledge; but I ask, why pain, if the same result could be achieved by unfeeling cogwheels, or computations? And I also ask, if particular gestalt experiences contribute to behaviour, can they engage with other 'cogwheels' so as to contribute *automatically*, or do they require a subject to experience them and respond?

Cairns-Smith's analogy of evolution is interesting; but unless and until a satisfactory account can be given of the place of conscious feelings in the generation of behaviour, evolutionary explanations of the emergence of consciousness will be deficient; and the use of the analogy of evolution to illuminate the development of an autonomous human personality will likewise be deficient.

In my article, I said that each person is the same in respect of capacity to choose, and Cairns-Smith says this sounds odd. But all I am saying is that every difference between persons is embodied (or at least reflected) in physical differences that affect the alternatives available and their respective probabilities; and although each person has the capacity to select from available alternatives, there are no *further* differences between persons beyond those embodied or reflected in their physical differences.

I am indebted to Cairns-Smith for the beautiful quotation from Shakespeare's Iago. My position, however, is that there is no gardener distinct from the garden: *the garden must cultivate itself.*

T.W. Clark

I am particularly grateful to Tom Clark for providing a response to my paper that forcefully expresses a version of the mechanistic viewpoint favoured by many, perhaps most, scientists and philosophers.

A central disagreement I have with him concerns his use of the expression 'black box' as applying to my account of free will. It suggests that I am proposing that, in the production of choices, there operates a discrete system, as to which no explanation is or can be given of what happens inside it, whereas a complete explanation can be given of the inputs to this system and of what happens to the outputs of the system. I think this misapprehends my account in two important ways.

First, Clark's black box terminology attributes to my account a separation, into discrete parts, of one element of choice-making that is mechanistic and another distinct element that is not mechanistic, a separation that my account in fact strongly rejects. I say that choice-making can be considered as an exercise of informal rationality, and thereby understood as a process in which a rational agent makes a choice on the basis of reasons that were, prior to the choice, inconclusive. Alternatively, choice-making can be considered as if it were a mechanistic process, either in terms of physical processes evolving in accordance with laws of nature, or in terms of computation-like algorithms. However, if my position is correct, any mechanistic approach to choice-making can at best explain what alternatives are available and give numerical probabilities, and must treat the occurrence of just one of the alternatives as a matter of chance within those probability parameters. I certainly do not suggest a 'black box' that determines which alternative occurs, after mechanistic processes run out. Rather, I say that the mechanistic approach gives an incomplete account of a whole process that can best be understood in terms of a choice made for reasons.

Second, Clark's approach suggests I am proposing something wholly inexplicable and incapable of being understood, whereas I fact I say we are very familiar with and have a reasonable understanding of informal rationality; and I would also contend that this understanding can be further developed and improved. Clark himself suggests that our rational processes are 'perhaps only fully understood at the representational, not physical, level'; and it is clear that, except in so far as our rational processes are algorithmic at the representational level, at that level those processes are indeterministic because premisses do not wholly constrain conclusions. The difference between his position and mine on this point is not that I propose some mysterious black box that takes over where algorithms run out, but rather that I suggest that our informal rationality, which (as Clark and I agree) we understand pretty well at the representational level, is truly explanatory and causally efficacious; whereas Clark seems to say that it merely supervenes on some underlying mechanistic process that we do not fully understand (Clark's black box?).

Another important disagreement between us arises from Clark's suggestion that the conscious self is but one of the contents of consciousness. Now, I accept that many of us may be fundamentally mistaken as to the nature of the subject of experience, for example in so far as we take this subject to be distinct from associated brain processes and/or to have continuity and stability and capacity to be active; and that some of our ideas about these matters may be no more than fallible contents of consciousness. But the idea that experiences are had by a subject (rather than being somehow 'free-floating') is so deeply presupposed and embedded in our language and in our ways of thinking that to deny this, without proposing a language concerning experiences that does not have this presupposition, is nonsense. In our language, 'pain' means 'pain as experienced by some feeler of pain' and cannot be understood in any other way; and the same goes for any other references to and descriptions of conscious experiences.

It could be argued that our language is in this respect not adequate to accurately reflect or describe reality; but Clark makes no suggestion as to why this might be so, much less any plausible proposal for a new language that does a better job. In fact the only faintly plausible strategy that has been proposed for talking and thinking about experiences in a way that does not presuppose a subject that has the experiences, is the suggestion that experiences are useful fictions. (This seems to be Dennett's position.) This avoids the contradiction of asserting there are experiences but denying there is a subject; but does so at the cost of denying that there really are experiences — that is, denying that there really are contents of consciousness.

Turning to more specific points, I do not suggest that volitional causation is special to human agents. Rather, I say that there is volitional causation wherever there is consciousness; although I also say that free will, as generally understood, requires rationality of the order of that possessed by human agents.

I do not overlook 'the possibility that (eg) pain has a particular subjective feel because of the functional and representational roles of the neural states that constitute it'; but I do consider it highly implausible. I believe this possibility is the merest speculation, in the absence of any account of how or why algorithmic computations could involve subjective feelings such as pain, or of what would distinguish algorithmic computations that involved such feelings from algorithmic computations that did not involve such feelings. Further, it is close to being disproved by scientific work on such things as phantom limbs and synaesthesia, where feelings occur in the absence of their usual causal roles.

I do not say, as Clark suggests, that choice is determined by the self and not by the reasons. I say that neither the self nor the reasons (nor indeed both of them together) *pre*-determine the choice, but that the subject and the reasons together determine the choice (by the subject making the choice for the reasons). It is a self-refuting fallacy to say that, if reasons are non-conclusive, there is no reason why the self reaches the choice it does — self-refuting because to deny the rationality of all reasoning apart from reasoning in which the reasons are conclusive is to deny the rationality of all informal reasoning, and thus to deny the supportability of most of our beliefs. I accept that it is possible that our informal reasoning is supported by processes that are algorithmic/computational, but we certainly do not *know* that this is so; and in order to have any confidence in our beliefs, we must accept the rationality of our informal reasoning, whether or not it is supported by algorithmic/computational processes. And of course I do not suggest that the rules of formal reasoning are unimportant — only that they do not account for all human rationality.

I do not deny that very often, perhaps most of the time, people find reasons for acting well (or badly) to be compelling, so that action in accordance with those reasons follows almost inevitably. The circumstance that the likelihood of any different action may be near zero (whether considered in terms of a numerical probability derived from physical laws, or some more generally understood likelihood based on a high-level agent-centred account) does not mean these actions are not freely chosen.

Clark claims that any indeterministic slack between the influence of reasons and behavioural output would decrease the efficacy of goal-directed action. This of course presupposes that our informal rationality depends entirely on computational algorithms — which might be the case, but is not certainly so and is contrary to my contentions. In my paper I give a specific reason why 'indeterministic slack' may contribute to efficacy, a reason which Clark does not address — namely, that it leaves room for a conscious organism to respond appropriately to particular gestalt experiences, grasped as a whole, and not merely to general features that can engage with natural laws or computational algorithms.

Clark says that to compete against mainstream evolutionary explanations, I 'must explain precisely how evolution installed the black box of free will and what indispensable function it serves'. This is a bit rich, when the mainstream explanations have totally failed to explain what installed subjective consciousness or what function it serves, whereas my account does at least propose a function for consciousness.

Clark suggests I say that the totality of the way a person is does not determine the outcome, whereas in fact I say that it does not *pre*-determine the outcome: as noted above, I say that the outcome is determined by the subject choosing on the basis of reasons. And in focussing on the capacity to select as being *the* determinant, Clark is again misconstruing my position: I say as plainly as I can that the capacity to select, as to which we are all the same, is not a severable part of the totality of the way we are; and I certainly do not say that the 'us' that provides the clincher is unaffected by differences between different persons. The clincher is provided by the totality choosing on the basis of the reasons.

R. Gomatam

Early in his comment, Ravi Gomatam says this:

> This immediately raises a difficulty with Hodgson's position. His opening stance that his plain-person-view of free will is incompatible with the determinism of classical physics would be true only if he also considers deterministic physics to give the full story about all causation that there is. Hodgson clearly doesn't believe in this, since he thinks volitional causation is over and beyond physical causation. These two stances appear contradictory.

I find this puzzling. Classical physics is generally seen as purporting to give deterministic laws of universal application, that operate in the real world so as to prescribe a unique path of development for any actual physical situation; and this surely is incompatible with a plain person's view of free will. So on that basis, my 'opening stance' is true; and the fact that I don't believe classical physics gives the full story about causation does not contradict this stance.

Gomatam supports the view that the scientific law is a short-hand way of representing regularities amidst our experiences, and that the identity between the 'physical object' (presumably, any object described by any physical theory) and the corresponding 'common-sense object' is not perfect; and he argues that accordingly even the determinism of classical physics is not incompatible with non-deterministic non-random free will. Of course, once one rejects any claim of classical physics that its laws exactly correspond with laws operating in the real world, this is correct. However, I do believe that there are natural laws operating in the real world, to which the laws proposed in physical theories approximate ever more closely as theories are developed and improved; and it is appropriate to consider how ideas about free will can relate to the operation of these real laws in the real world, even though we do not know and may never know these real laws with absolute precision.

I agree with Gomatam that my first three propositions are necessary but not sufficient conditions for conscious free will; but I do not think that quantum theory shows that the second and third of them apply to all physical systems. I believe however that my first five propositions together give conditions that are sufficient as well as necessary for conscious free will.

G. Gomes

I take issue with Gilberto Gomes where he says that I believe 'free will is incompatible with natural causation'. I say rather that natural causation is not limited to the evolution of systems as determined by laws of nature coupled with randomness; that is, I say that choice is part of natural causation, as proposed by my proposition 5.

Gomes also asserts that 'if conscious processes of free will are another aspect of physical processes of the brain, it is hard to see how they could escape being subject to physical causation.' But I don't say that they do escape: I say that physical causation limits the available alternatives, and also the reasons on the basis of which choices are made. Just as the physical aspect of the process imposes constraints not fully explicable in terms of the conscious aspect, the conscious aspect can by choice impose constraints not fully explicable in terms of the physical aspect.

He also says I believe 'that physical determinism plus randomness cannot account for "the subject's particular gestalt experiences that are part of the pre-choice state"'. I do not say this. As explained in some detail in Hodgson (2002), I believe that laws plus randomness do account for, in the sense of *giving rise to*, particular gestalt experiences. What I say is that these particular gestalt experiences cannot themselves then engage with laws, and that accordingly QM statistics cannot *take into account* such experiences as wholes, and laws and randomness cannot account for all their effects.

I entirely agree with Gomes that conscious judgment may be a naturally caused non-algorithmic process. But if Gomes accepts that this is so, he needs to explain how a process can be wholly determined by rules and randomness, and yet be both rational and non-algorithmic. It may be the case that our informal rationality is based on law-governed processes that we do not understand, selected through millions of years of evolution — but if so, such processes would in my book be algorithmic.

I also agree with Gomes that 'our control' may be included in antecedent natural causes. What I say is that there are powerful reasons for thinking that *the way our control is exercised* is not itself simply a function of our pre-choice state plus laws of nature and randomness.

L. Jaswal

Liberty Jaswal argues that I fail to address the challenge arising from the 'constraint within QM ... that the character in which an event occurs must be random'; and that because I stipulate that choice is non-random, my account of free will violates QM by definition.

It is true that standard *interpretations* of QM assert that events occur at random within probability parameters; but there are other 'hidden variable' interpretations, notably that of David Bohm, that assert that randomness is only apparent, the appearance being caused by limitations on what we can know. My approach would challenge standard interpretations in so far as they suggest that QM *requires* randomness; and also 'hidden variable' interpretations, in so far as they suggest that the underlying reality is deterministic.

What I say is that, if one accepts that QM can do no more than give the best available account of how systems develop over time, based on the application of rules to physical features, then no violation of QM is involved in an account that says that what is chosen will be possible according to QM, and will tend to conform to QM statistics, with any deviation from those statistics being explained by the ability of the choosing system to take account of gestalts with which no rules (QM or otherwise) can engage.

R. Kane

As Robert Kane says, there is much that he and I agree on. However, there may be an important difference between us concerning my proposition 5, and its relationship to randomness and to conformity to physical laws. This may in turn give rise to somewhat different approaches to the question of agent causation, although I don't have any significant disagreement with what Kane says on this topic in his response.

In my article, I suggest that it is an important and positive feature of our rationality that it is indeterministic; and that outcomes that are chosen could be more advantageous than outcomes that occur randomly in accordance with QM statistics. Kane says this would mean that choices must fail to conform to the statistical laws of QM. I said much the same in my target article, but I now think this is incorrect. Statistics only give a high probability that results (say, 'yes' or 'no') will conform to certain proportions, and say nothing about which occasions will have one result ('yes') and which will have the other ('no'). Non-random selection could give a higher likelihood that the result 'yes' will occur on those occasions when 'yes' would be advantageous, and that the result 'no' will occur on those occasions when 'no' would be advantageous, without necessarily altering their proportions. Certainly, I contend, a demonstrated departure from QM statistics is unlikely in the extreme, because the felt strength of reasons is likely to reflect QM probabilities, and because of the complexity and uniqueness of pre-choice states (see Hodgson, 1999).

However, I accept that my position makes a choice-caused deviation from QM statistics possible; and I argue that this would not be a violation of physical laws but a limitation on their applicability. Against this, Kane argues that, if there were such a limitation, there must then be further physical laws that do apply, which will themselves be either deterministic or statistical.

In relation to this, what I suggest is that there may be different types of physical laws — that there may be not only laws that constrain outcomes (laws of constraint), but also laws that determine in what circumstances physical systems can select outcomes from those left available by the laws of constraint (laws of empowerment). There may also be laws that assist or guide systems in making their selections (laws of guidance). My suggestion is that consciousness and capacity to select are two sides of the same coin, emerging in evolution and in the development of individual systems just as determined by laws of empowerment. Laws of guidance would be at best dimly grasped by primitive conscious systems, but grasped progressively more completely as the rationality of conscious systems increases. No doubt some would call this panicky metaphysics; but before they do so, I would ask that they carefully read the two articles (Hodgson, 2001; 2002) in which I introduce and develop these ideas. I suggest that these ideas are plausible and have considerable explanatory power, although of course they themselves raise further questions.

So, when I talk about a limitation on the applicability of the laws of QM, what I am saying is that the those laws may give the best possible explanation of outcomes based on all features with which laws of constraint can engage, by way of determining what outcomes are possible, and giving an indication of their numerical probabilities that is the best possible on the basis of those features. However, I argue that no laws can engage with gestalt features of particular experiences: and that if, as seems to me highly plausible, such features enter into the making of conscious choices, their contribution cannot be determined by any rules. This contribution can only be understood as one element (and *not* a severable element) in the plausible reasoning of a conscious subject.

N. Maxwell

There is also much about which Nicholas Maxwell and I agree, but there are areas of fundamental disagreement.

One such area concerns the formulation of problems. I am extremely wary of saying categorically what are *the* fundamental problems in various areas of philosophy, including free will. There are many problems and many issues, and I think it is often a mistake to say that some are fundamental and others are not. It may be that investigation does show that some problems are more fundamental than others; but I am doubtful whether we can yet make that judgment about the various problems and issues concerning free will discussed by Maxwell.

I certainly do not assume that *the* central philosophical issue about free will is whether or not it is compatible with determinism, although I do believe this is one important issue. I believe that another important issue is what if any versions of free will are compatible with what modern science tells us about the world. However, I do not agree with Maxwell that this is *the* proper way to formulate the problem. It is one issue alongside and related to the free will / determinism issue, and both issues are important.

I believe that the possibility that the universe is physically comprehensible, in the sense that everything that we experience, think and do has a complete physical explanation, requiring no mention of our intentions, desires and decisions, is a threat to free will; but I do not agree with Maxwell that it is *the real* threat. There are other important threats, including I believe threats associated with acceptance of determinism (or the combination of determinism and randomness) and with dilemmas about responsibility such as those powerfully put by Galen Strawson.

Maxwell's first suggested characterization of free will (FW1) is as the capacity to realize (that is, to apprehend or make real) what is of value in a range of circumstances. He says this capacity can be misused; and indeed I would contend that in fact any plausibility of identifying this capacity with free will depends on a tacit assumption that a person having this capacity can exercise it so as to realize what is of value to a greater or lesser extent, or not at all. It is this assumed flexibility, or availability of choice, in the exercise of this capacity, not the realizing of what is of value as such, that links this capacity to free will. What identifying free will with this capacity does is essentially to limit the concept to areas where its exercise may be of moral (or perhaps aesthetic) significance. It does not contribute to the resolution of issues such as whether free will is compatible with determinism or with what science tells us, or how to draw the line between what if anything we are truly responsible for and what we are not responsible for.

Maxwell's second characterization of free will (FW2) is as control by our authentic self of our inner and outer actions; so that those actions are free which are correctly explained as being produced and guided by this authentic self. I think the idea of control carries with it the idea of being able to direct actions as we choose, and that again any plausibility of this characterization depends heavily upon the tacit assumption of the availability of choice. Further, I think that the notion of an authentic self is unsatisfactory in that it is either circular and vacuous or else excludes important cases from being exercises of free will. Take for example a decision to reform. A person's long history of wrongdoing may be such that his or her 'authentic self' must be considered one that overvalues the fruits of wrongdoing and undervalues the worth of a good life. If that person decides to reform, there may be nothing in the person's history prior to this choice that would justify describing the decision as an exercise of control by the person's authentic self. If it be contended that the person's authentic self is that which is manifested by the decision to reform, this would make circular and vacuous the identification of authentic selves for the purpose of determining whether free action is occurring.

Maxwell says it is 'wildly implausible' to suggest that physical events occur that cannot be fully explained physically. I do indeed suggest this: I say that the physical explanations of conscious choices can only go so far as to give the available alternatives and the probability parameters for each of them, while explanations in terms of a choice made for reasons by a conscious agent can give an understanding why one of the alternatives occurred rather than any of the others. Indeed, I say that the choice does actually do what physical processes considered as such cannot do, namely determine which of the alternatives actually does occur. Maxwell says this is wildly implausible because it would mean that evolutionary processes (being presumably, until the appearance of conscious agents, processes in which there can be no incompleteness of physical explanations) lead (with the appearance of conscious agents) to the occurrence of physical events that do not have a full physical explanation.

This is an aspect of the problem of *emergence*, which is indeed a difficult one; but its difficulties are not peculiar to incompatibilist versions of free will. There is the parallel problem of how physical processes, fully describable in an objective and third-person way, give rise through evolution to conscious processes, which are adequately describable only by reference to a subjective first-person point of view. And Maxwell's own version of compatibilism faces a similar problem (albeit perhaps in a milder form), namely how it is that physical processes give rise to physical events that constitute or correspond with human actions, which actions themselves can be adequately explained only by way of what Maxwell calls personalistic explanations — that is, explanations in terms of experiences, beliefs and so on, which according to Maxwell can be intelligible, true, and irreducible to physical explanations. Maxwell addresses this problem at some length in Maxwell (2001).

I think that, if there are such personalistic explanations of human actions, as Maxwell contends, it is by no means implausible to suggest that they may add something to the explanation of the physical events to which the human actions correspond or correlate, and indeed that what the personalistic explanations describe may actually contribute to the causation of these events. In my target article and in other articles referred to in it, I give substantial positive reasons for believing that this is the case. Maxwell does not address these reasons, so his assertion of implausibility is given little support.

Maxwell concludes with a remark to the effect that I have not shown that my incompatibilist version of free will is more worth having than compatibilist versions of FW1 or FW2.

My purpose in my article was not to show that my version of free will is more worth having than other versions. Rather, it was to give an elaboration of what I took to be a plain person's idea of free will, so as to make it philosophically and scientifically respectable — and to consider whether it was plausible as compared with other views. Maxwell has said that my version is implausible, and his last remark may be taken as suggesting that plausible compatibilist versions of free will (either FW1 or FW2) adequately reflect the plain person's view, or at least capture what is worthwhile in the plain person's view. Now I have already identified what I see as particular shortcomings with FW1 and FW2, notably that both gain plausibility because of an unstated assumption that choice is involved, that FW1 does no more than restrict the concept to areas of moral significance, and that the notion of authentic self in FW2 is unsatisfactory.

In addition, there is in my opinion a general problem with all theories that make free will compatible with acceptance of the view that all physical occurrences have complete physical explanations, to which personalistic explanations add nothing; namely, that this precludes any reasonable attributions of responsibility to persons, and in particular allocations of responsibility as between things that are in no sense up to us (our genes, our early upbringing, other environmental factors) and things that are in some sense at least up to us (our choices).

Galen Strawson argues forcefully that the way we act at any time is the result of the way we are at that time; that we cannot be truly responsible for the way we act at any time unless we are, to some extent at least, responsible for the way we are at that time; and that we cannot be to any extent responsible for the way we are unless we have been responsible for the way we have acted in the past — so we can never become responsible for the way we are or the way we act. In my opinion, if the physical events of the way we act are either determined uniquely by prior physical events and laws of nature, or else occur randomly within probability parameters that are so determined, there is no plausible answer to this argument. No distinction could be drawn between the hand of cards we are dealt by our genes and environment, and the way this hand is played. Life's game would be like clock patience. I do not say that life's game is like bridge, because that would suggest a dualism of players being distinct from the cards: I say rather that the cards, or some of them, play themselves, though not automatically or mechanistically.

I think it is only if choice contributes to what is determined by the existing hand of cards that Strawson's dilemma can be overcome; so that it becomes possible to say that, yes, this person's actions were influenced by and partly caused by genes and environment, but they were also partly the person's choice, which itself was not fully pre-determined by genes and environment. It then becomes possible to say that the person is responsible, but the degree of responsibility (for good or ill) may be more or less, because of the influence of genes and environment. This is, I believe, part of a plain person's view of free will, and an important part that is not captured by any compatibilist view.

J.J.C. Smart

In his comments, J.J.C. Smart raises questions about the definitions of determinism and chance, and also about the intelligibility of a positive characterization of free will that is neither determinism nor chance.

I fully agree with him that it would be wrong to equate determinism with predictability. I adopt a conception of determinism as involving the unique determination of what happens by prior conditions and laws of nature, and I think this conception is clear enough for the purposes of the free will debate. There can be disagreement about details, and no doubt there are technical issues I am skating over, but I believe this is similar in substance to the model theoretic approach that Smart endorses.

As for chance, my conception is that chance obtains where (1) prior conditions and laws of nature do not uniquely determine what happens, but determine only alternatives and probability parameters, and (2) what actually happens is the occurrence of one of these alternatives, with *nothing else* contributing to the determination of which alternative it is. As I understand it, this is broadly the conception of chance or randomness adopted in the standard approach to quantum mechanics (QM).

My positive conception of free will is that, as with chance, prior conditions and laws of nature determine alternatives and probability parameters, but (unlike chance) something else *does* contribute to the determination of what actually happens. This something else is not a separate or severable something just added on to the determination of alternatives and probability parameters, but rather an integral part of a whole process of conscious decision-making or acting, to which the determination of alternatives and probability parameters contributes, and by which one of the alternatives is selected. In this process, the person or other agent exercising free will may resolve inconclusive and incommensurable reasons supporting different alternatives. This positive conception is elaborated throughout my target article, particularly in relation to proposition 5.

Smart very quickly dismisses my contention that the non-locality of QM is required for the perception of gestalts, apparently because the span of the specious present is sufficient to accommodate communication between all parts of the brain involved in such perceptions. In Hodgson (1996) I said this about this argument:

> In TMM at p. 384, I dealt with this by pointing out that our awareness of different aspects of viewed objects is not sequential: for example, if we see something even as simple as a red circle, the circleness and the redness are inextricably together, not successive, even though it seems clear that circle-detecting neurons are spatially separated from red-detecting neurons. So unless one supposes that it is all brought together in some red-circle- detecting neuron — which seems just about as unlikely as the once-postulated 'grandmother neuron', which was supposed to fire whenever one recognised one's grandmother — one needs nonlocality to explain the all-at-once awareness of the red circle.
>
> I still think this is a good argument, but the approach of this section permits another and broader argument. Granted that the psychological present has duration, it is still grasped as a whole, with co-consciousness of many elements: for example, a stable visual scene with both co-present properties and sequential changes, and slabs of auditory sequences such as spoken words or melodies. All these elements, corresponding to many events in different parts of the brain occurring during the relevant slab of time, are bracketed or chunked in the conscious experience. If our

brains were systems which, for all practical purposes, operated on the basis of local causes obeying the requirements of relativity theory, then this bracketing or chunking by the brain itself would at best be superfluous and epiphenomenal — and an outside observer's suggestion that this bracketing or chunking was performed in or by the system itself would be gratuitous, and eliminable by Occam's razor.

I remain of this view. Of course, if one takes the position that the experience of gestalts is epiphenomenal (or, as Dennett would have it, fictional), then non-locality is not required. Otherwise, I believe, it is required.

Smart then focuses on my suggested classification of laws of nature. I do not agree that, in my classification, only C-laws express regularities. I say that all three classes express regularities of different kinds. In the case of C-laws, the regularities are those of constraint; in the case of E-laws, the regularities are those of empowerment; in the case of G-laws, the regularities are those of guidance. Thus, I would argue, E-laws are such that, whenever certain conditions are satisfied, there is a subject with the capacity to experience and act. Smart suggests that to postulate laws that are, like G-laws, in effect in the imperative mood, is to appeal to the supernatural or at least to retreat to a pre-scientific view of what laws of nature are. Plainly I have a wider conception of what is or may be natural than does Smart. And I believe that the wrongness of some things (such as torturing children for amusement) is more than a reflection of an evolutionary artefact and that there must, accordingly, be some kind of natural imperatives existing alongside the scientific laws of nature.

I disagree strongly with Smart's suggestion that consciousness is awareness of awareness, with mere awareness being when we are on 'automatic pilot'. I believe that consciousness involves the interdependent existence of a subject and contents of consciousness (that is, in general terms, a combination of subject-and-experiences), and that the qualitative 'feel' of the experiences to the subject is an important feature of consciousness. Whenever I actually feel pain, I contend, I am neither on automatic pilot nor just monitoring some other first-order 'awareness': I am feeling something having a distinctive quality, and I am conscious of this experience, whether or not I enter into any second-order monitoring of what I am feeling.

I also disagree strongly with Smart's suspicion of 'psychocentrism'. There is of course a sense in which conscious systems like human beings may be 'small beer in the cosmic scheme of things', namely in terms of physical quantities like size, mass, energy, distance, and so on. Yet even in purely physical terms, size isn't everything; and it is widely accepted that the human brain is the most complex physical system known in the universe. More importantly, I think there is a vast difference between a universe without observers and a universe with observers. Although I don't agree with those idealist thinkers who say that we can only conceive of a universe as observed, so that an unobserved universe is inconceivable, I do say that a universe without observers would be pointless in a way that our universe is not. In addition, there is the possibility suggested by QM that participation of observers is an essential feature of our universe; and there is also the view of many thinkers that the universe happens to be fined-tuned in just such a way as to permit the emergence of conscious intelligence. I think it is reasonable to believe that consciousness is very important in the scheme of things.

As regards the evolutionary selection of consciousness, Smart agrees that we have heightened consciousness when in a crisis, such as being approached by a man-eating tiger; but he suggests this is because there are advantages in monitoring one's awareness. I disagree: I think the heightened consciousness is of *what is going on around us*, and of *possibilities for action in the world* that may avoid or minimise the danger, rather than any monitoring of our own awareness, which would seem to be of little direct benefit in the circumstances.

I'm not sure what part of my article Smart is referring to when he says I elucidate free will as being guided by reasons as opposed to causes. In fact, I believe reasons, or at least reasons-as-apprehended-by-a-subject, are causes of a kind; but that they are different from physical causes particularly because they are inconclusive and often incommensurable, and have causal efficacy only in so far as they are given effect to through the decisions or actions of conscious subjects. Physical causes, on the other hand, operate automatically, and in their totality conclusively, so as to bring about either a unique result or (where chance or free will is relevant) a situation where there are alternatives with determined probabilities, just one of which occurs.

Smart endorses a weak kind of fatalism, based on the four-dimensional world of relativity in which the future exists tenselessly, just as real as the past. I think the jury is out on that one: although it seems that quantum non-locality cannot be used to support faster-than-light communications, quantum non-locality does suggest that there may be simultaneity of space-like separated events according to some preferred frame of reference (see Davies and Brown 1986 at 48-50, Bell 1987); and thus it suggests that, although the four-dimensional world of relativity may remain a useful model, it does not fully capture the true relationship between space and time.

Finally, Smart suggests that compatibilist theories of punishment may be more humane than retributive theories, and in any event we are concerned with truth not morality. I have discussed in Hodgson (1998) and (2000) what I see as problems for wholly utilitarian theories of punishment; and although I agree that this does not directly impact on questions of the truth of the plain person's conception of free will and responsibility, I do think it does bear on questions of the onus and standard of proof. I think this plain person's conception is important in the defence of human rights, and that it should not be dismissed without convincing proof — which is not yet forthcoming.

S.A. Spence

I agree with Sean A. Spence that, if philosophers wish to address the basis of will, they will increasingly need to understand neurobiology. However, I contend that, if neurobiologists wish to draw conclusions from neurobiology as to the efficacy, or non-efficacy, of what feel to be conscious choices, they should attend carefully to the reasoning by which they draw those conclusions, and to philosophical considerations that may bear on that reasoning.

In his response to my paper, Spence seems to suggest that demonstration that brain function imposes 'constraints' on our choices, or that choices are not 'independent' of brain function or of genes, would be contrary to my position – whereas in fact my position fully accepts those propositions. Spence seems to concede this at one point, but then elsewhere seems to disregard it.

I do not, as Spence suggests, equate an experience with *its own* causation. Our feeling of making a choice is an aspect of physical-and-mental processes that have causal antecedents in prior processes – although I suggest that these prior processes only pre-determine the available alternatives and their probabilities. The progress of the choice and its outcome are contributed to by the choice-making itself; and to that extent (only), the choice-making (though not the *feeling* of choice-making) can be considered as causing itself. However, as I have said a number of times in these responses, I certainly do not propose that there is 'something special which sits at the end of the causal chain, which makes the decision'; rather, I say that the choosing subject is a totality, having features with which causal laws can engage, but also (and inseverably) having a capacity to choose.

I did not undertake in my paper to give a critique of opposing views, but rather to give a clear statement of the plain person's view (which is essentially my view); so it is perhaps understandable that my critique of opposing views might be seen as cursory. To my mind, Spence's critique of my position is cursory in that it does not squarely address the main support for my position and the main shortcoming in mechanistic views such as his own, namely the problem of explaining consciousness and its function(s). Spence's main argument against my position is to the effect that the feeling of conscious choice is merely a feeling that accompanies the mechanistic working out of physical processes that preceded it. But if this is right, then what function does consciousness have? All Spence can suggest is that 'its role may be to acquaint us with what has just occurred, and thereby to influence (through feedback mechanisms) what is next to be done'. Let us look a little more closely at this.

The words 'acquaint us' suggest that the 'feedback mechanisms' may involve some contribution from 'us'; but if so, why and how could this contribution be any different from the contribution 'we' make at the time of action, that is, in Spence's opinion, no more than an illusory feeling, accompanying the mechanistic working out of physical processes? To put this another way, if 'we' can make a contribution, by way of some kind of choice or decision, to the operation of feedback mechanisms, this means there must be something about conscious processes that makes them more than a reflection of the working out of physical processes; and there is then no reason why that 'something' cannot be active, as it feels to be, at the time of actual decisions and actions.

So it would seem that, despite the words 'acquaint us', Spence is really talking about some automatic process that involves no element of choice or decision. But if so, what role does consciousness have in such an automatic process? Does it operate by engaging with laws other than the ordinary laws of physics, and if so what laws? And if they are laws additional to physical laws, what room do the physical laws leave for their operation? Does consciousness operate otherwise than through computational algorithms that are carried out in accordance with the operation of physical laws on the system carrying out those algorithms? If so, why and how? If not, what contribution does consciousness make to the performance of algorithms?

I believe that, to be coherent, Spence has to deny a role for consciousness, even in feedback mechanisms; and his views, like most mechanistic views, ultimately collapse into epiphenomenalism. Like many neuroscientists, Spence is strong and persuasive when giving an account of neural mechanisms, but to my mind wholly unconvincing when trying to explain consciousness and its role in our behaviour.

Turning to Libet, I do not suggest that a choice between doing something and doing nothing is trivial. However, it is different from cases where two or more alternative actions are being actively considered. And although Spence says the 'same effect' can be seen in such cases, I do not understand him to be saying that physical changes observed prior to the feeling of making the choice indicate *which* alternative will be chosen. That could be damaging to my position. But I understand Spence to be saying merely that, prior to the choice, physical processes can be observed that correlate to choosing *when* to act and other physical processes can be observed that correlate to choosing *which way* to act; and that does no harm to my position.

Even in the case where the choice is between doing something and doing nothing, the role of consciousness is not excluded. A conscious decision is made to press a button at some time in the future. Pursuant to that decision, brain activity later occurs, that makes immediately available the alternatives of pressing the button or not doing so. Since a decision to press was made earlier, it is very unlikely that the alternative of not pressing will be chosen. The conscious process in effect confirms that the pressing is to go ahead. One does not look for some separate brain process that might explain a veto, if it occurred — in the unlikely case that a choice is made not to go ahead with the pressing, it is one of the alternatives made available by the same brain activity that made available the alternative of immediately pressing the button.

H.P. Stapp

Henry Stapp makes two main points in his comment on my article: first, he argues that choice should be located squarely in the particular QM process that von Neumann called Process 1; and second, he challenges my suggestion that choices cannot be accounted for by strict rules of any kind. I will consider these in turn.

In my article, I say that, according to QM, any indeterminism is mere randomness. Stapp rightly points out that, in the von Neumann formulation of QM, there is at least the potential for indeterminism that is not mere randomness. This is because, in that formulation, QM has three processes: the deterministic development of a system in accordance with the Schroedinger equation, the Process 1 probing of the system, and the random occurrence of one of the possible outcomes. And as Stapp points out, there are no presently known laws that govern choices concerning what Process 1 probing is to be undertaken; and such choices can strongly influence the course of physical events. A good example of this is the quantum Zeno (or 'watched pot never boils') effect: frequent measurements of a quantum system can reduce to near-zero the chances of a change occurring within a certain time, which otherwise would have significant probability if the system were measured only at the end of that time. Stapp postulates that experiential qualities enter in a non-redundant and non-eliminable way into Process 1 choices, and in that way significantly affect what happens.

This is an approach that is generally consistent with my position, although my understanding of QM and of the brain is insufficient for me either to reject it or to wholly embrace it.

One difficulty I have with Stapp's approach is that it may require some lack of correlation between Process 1 choices and physical processes in the brain. To be consistent, Stapp should I think accept that physical processes in the brain are themselves subject to QM, in its three aspects. If the transition from the pre-choice state to the post-choice state in Process 1 choices did correlate wholly with such processes, it would seem that these choices themselves must be caused by some combination of deterministic development, prior Process 1 choices and random outcomes — and *those* Process 1 choices would be similarly caused, and so on. Any 'non-redundant and non-eliminable' role for experiential qualities would then seem to be pushed indefinitely into the past and thus effectively excluded. On the other hand, if the transition process in Process 1 choices does not correlate with physical processes themselves subject to QM, in its three aspects, then a question arises as to why only Process 1 choices, and not other elements of the subject's volitional decision or action, have this lack of correlation with physical processes subject to QM.

Accordingly, at present I prefer to take a broader view, and not to commit to associating choice with von Neumann's Process 1, rather than any other process not required by QM to be deterministic.

Stapp suggests that it is inconsistent with QM to treat as non-random any process that according to QM is random. However, I would argue that it is inconsistent only with certain interpretations of QM; and I see my position rather as accepting that QM (and subsequent developments of quantum theory) tells us everything that can be gleaned from physical quantities, but cannot tell us about the impact of non-physical properties. It can tells us what alternatives are available, and give probabilities for them; but those probabilities are themselves based solely on physical quantities and conceivably could be affected by experiential qualities that QM can say nothing about. In particular, since QM can only apply to general physical quantities, it cannot say anything about what if any effect unique experiential gestalts may have. Thus, I see my position not as being inconsistent with QM, but rather as saying it cannot tell us everything.

Stapp's second point has two aspects. First, he suggests that, unless the selection process is governed by strict rules, it could not produce pertinent determinate actions and beliefs. And second, he argues that personal responsibility is rooted in the immediate causes of an agent's actions, and in particular that 'it stems from the capacity of the agent to grasp and understand the consequences of its actions, and from its physical capacity to act in accordance with the freedom accorded to it by its inner nature, and in particular by the *qualitative process* that allows its actions to be controlled by sufficient willful effort'.

My initial reaction to this was to think that Stapp was arguing for a form of compatibilism of responsibility with determinism. However, on further reflection, I now do not think this is so. Rather, I suspect that any difference between us relates to our understanding of what it is for a selection process to be governed by strict rules.

I see my position as consistent with extensive philosophical literature that tends to support the view that human rationality transcends conformity with rules, including the work on induction by Hume, Popper, Hempel, Goodman and others; critiques of attempts such as those by Carnap to formalise plausible reasoning; Goedel's theorem and Penrose's development of it; Quine on indeterminacy of translation and Wittgenstein on rule-following; and Putnam's arguments to the conclusion that human rationality cannot be formalised without formalising complete human psychology, and possibly not even then. This literature is not conclusive, and there remains the possibility that human rationality depends on evolution-selected computation-like processes; but the alternative view that I adopt does not deserve to be summarily dismissed.

In addition, in my arguments concerning proposition 5, which Stapp does not address, I have put forward positive reasons for thinking that this (that is, rationality that does not depend on conformity with rules) is just what consciousness is *for*; and also some suggestions as to how this is achieved. As I put it in Hodgson (2002):

> If rationality is partly explained by our ability to grasp particular whole experiences, then our beliefs may be justified by many factors going beyond consistency with other data according to rules of logic, probability, and mathematics. Properties of experiences such as immediacy, clarity, vividness and consistency can support belief as to the reality of the apparent objects of experience. Beliefs can also be supported by properties such as coherence, profuseness of support, and proximity and similarity to accepted beliefs. We can reason by analogy on the basis of unanalysable similarities and differences between some gestalts and others. Theories underlying beliefs can be supported by properties such as coherence (again), simplicity and beauty.

Stapp criticises my position on the basis that rules are necessary if selection is to produce pertinent actions and beliefs; but in a private communication he has said that he is not thinking about rules that are implementable in mechanistic ways.

This may mean that the rules which Stapp suggests must support rational choices are not dissimilar from what I call laws of guidance, these being laws that do not operate automatically to constrain outcomes but rather guide conscious systems in selecting outcomes. Stapp's communication continued:

> I am writing a paper with Kathy Laskey on plausible reasoning by quantum agents, based on the propagation of beliefs by Baysian inference. The rules are

nonmechanically and nonlocally implemented. I suspect that when it is worked out it will evade traditional philosophical arguments: various normal ideas about determinism will not hold, but there will be rules of a more general kind. I do not think that possibility deserves to be summarily dismissed.

This paper may clarify whether there is or is not any fundamental disagreement between us. Bayesian inference does follow rules that can be mechanically applied, but it depends on estimates of prior probabilities that cannot be mechanically arrived at. I have argued (Hodgson 1995) that such inference is best regarded as a useful check on the consistency of our estimates of probabilities, rather than as fully explaining or justifying informal reasoning. I remain of the view that informal reasoning may be guided by rules, but is not wholly determined by them.

Review Of My Propositions

There was little direct attack on proposition 1, the alternatives requirement. However, plainly Clark, Maxwell, Smart and Spence would contend that any indeterminism that may be suggested by QM has nothing to do with voluntary action; and Jaswal contended that QM *requires* any departure from determinism be random, not chosen. My view that the existence of alternatives is relevant to free will was supported by Gomatam, Gomes (I think), Kane and Stapp.

Proposition 2, the consciousness requirement, was attacked most strongly by Spence, who suggested that neuroscience showed that the real decisions occur prior to any conscious awareness that a decision is being made. I think this grossly overstates what is shown by experiments such as those by Libet, and also inevitably leads to epiphenomenalism, which in my opinion is highly implausible. Gomatam, Kane and Stapp supported the view that it is essential to free voluntary actions and choices that they be made consciously. This appears also to be supported by the compatibilism of Gomes and Maxwell.

Proposition 3, the grasping requirement, attracted little direct comment. I remain of the view that, unless a person grasps, at least to some minimum extent, the availability of an alternative, there is no exercise of free will (although there may still be responsibility, because the action is the result of prior exercises of free will); and also that when we are conscious, we generally do in fact grasp the availability of alternatives, if only the alternative of doing nothing.

To my mind, it is an important and striking feature of our reasoning that we are conscious of reasons, and that generally these reasons are inconclusive. This seems to me particularly obvious when there are competing reasons that are incommensurable, as is often the case with plausible reasoning about what to believe. This view, expressed in proposition 4, was supported by Kane, but hardly noticed by anyone else. To me, this was disappointing, but not altogether surprising. The existence of a gap between reasons and decision is I believe a major problem for deterministic or mechanistic views. If epiphenomenalism is to be avoided, reasons must be efficacious; but it is difficult, indeed I believe impossible, to ascribe an efficacious role for inconclusive reasons in a mechanistic or deterministic account of human conduct.

Clark attempted to turn this around by suggesting that my position is falsified because people find reasons compelling, and act in accordance with compelling reasons; and he also suggested that what is unformalizable at the phenomenal level may be formalizable at the machine or design levels. But compelling is not conclusive, and it is part of rationality that even compelling reasons can sometimes be ignored or defeated. And Clark does not explain how what is formalizable at the machine or design level can be both unformalizable and also efficacious at the phenomenal level.

Proposition 5, the selection requirement, was opposed particularly by Clark and Smart, with Clark focussing on what he called the 'black box' of decision-making, and Smart focussing on my suggested extension of the notion of a laws of nature, as well as on his difficulty in grasping a libertarian notion of free will. I need not add here to my comments on these objections, which in my opinion do not outweigh considerations in favour of proposition 5, particularly those numbered (1), (2), and (5) in my target article.

I was hoping for some direct consideration of the argument numbered (5), which as I mentioned in a footnote was introduced and developed in Hodgson (2001 and 2002). I find it compelling that there cannot be rules or laws that engage with whole gestalts, as distinct from their constituent features or parameters; so that if we can respond to whole gestalts, our response cannot be as pre-determined by rules or laws. For those who, like me, think that we probably can grasp and do respond to whole gestalts (such as a Schubert melody), this would both support indeterministic rationality and explain why such rationality could have advantages over procedures that depend entirely on computational algorithms. I would welcome debate on this.

Stapp seems sympathetic to my overall position, but suggests I go too far when I say that the selection process cannot be accounted for by strict rules of any kind. He suggests that rationality requires that decisions be determined by rules, albeit rules that are different from the local and mechanistic rules of classical mechanics; and that this does not preclude personal responsibility. At present, I do not see how rules that uniquely pre-determine the transition from one state of the world (S1) to another (S2) can be other than mechanistic, even if those rules engage with conscious mental features of S1; but it may be that further dialogue between us could bring our views closer together.

Kane agrees with proposition 5, though I'm unclear how this stands with his insistence that choices must conform to QM statistics. But again, I suspect that further dialogue may bring our views closer together.

Consistently with their views on other propositions, Clark, Smart and Spence suggest that in deterministic free will would require something supernatural, contrary to proposition 6. Jaswal and Kane suggest that my version conflicts with QM, although Kane, along with Gomatam and Stapp, consider that at least some version of indeterministic free will is consistent with physical science.

If proposition 5 is accepted, then it must be accepted that subjects have the capacity to make selections. My suggestion in proposition 7 that we are all alike in our capacity to select drew particular attack from Clark, and scepticism from

Cairns-Smith. However, as noted earlier, the essence of my position is that each totality that chooses is distinguished from other totalities only by features that engage with laws and thus affect the available alternatives and their respective probabilities.

Proposition 8, concerning moral principles, ventures into the question of whether moral requirements constitute or reflect some objective feature of the universe, or are merely evolution-generated human artefacts, or are some combination of the two. I have barely touched on this topic, and do not pretend to have done anything like justice to it; but I think that perhaps the plain person's theory of free will, coupled with my suggested classification of laws of nature, could provide a framework within which moral requirements could be seen as being objectively based, while having substantial flexibility in their detailed content and application. Although such a view is opposed by many philosophers, including Smart, I believe that the wrongness of some conduct is more than a reflection of an opinion which, for evolutionary reasons, is widely held but is otherwise baseless.

So lastly, do we have a measure of ultimate responsibility, as proposed by proposition 9? Not according to Clark, Smart and Spence, consistently with their comments on the other propositions. However, Kane and Stapp think we do; and Gomes contends his compatibilism leaves voluntary conduct 'under our control'. I am unpersuaded by this, but remain of the view we do have some ultimate responsibility for what we do.

Concluding Remarks

To my mind, the most interesting area for further consideration is that involving proposition 5. It may be that ongoing work on self-organization and non-linearity has some bearing on it; and certainly I would like to explore the possibility of rapprochement between my views and those of Kane and Stapp, and possibly also Gomes.

References

Bell, J. (1987), *Speakable and Unspeakable in Quantum Mechanics* (Cambridge: CUP).
Davies, P. and Brown, J.R. (1986), *The Ghost in the Atom* (Cambridge: Cambridge University Press).
Hameroff, S, *et al*, (ed. 1998), *Toward a Science of Consciousness II* (Cambridge MA: MIT).
Hodgson, D. (1995), 'Probability: The logic of the law — a response', *Oxford Journal of Legal Studies*, **14**, pp. 51–68.
Hodgson, D. (1996), 'Nonlocality, local indeterminism, and consciousness', *Ratio*, **9**, 1–22.
Hodgson, D. (1998), 'Folk psychology, science, and the criminal law', in Hameroff *et al.* (1998).
Hodgson, D. (1999), 'Hume's mistake', in Libet *et al.* (1999).
Hodgson, D. (2000), 'Guilty mind or guilty brain: criminal responsibility in the age of neuroscience', *The Australian Law Journal*, **74**, pp. 661–80.
Hodgson, D. (2001), 'Constraint, empowerment, and guidance: a conjectural classification of laws of nature', *Philosophy*, **76**, 341-70.
Hodgson, D. (2002), 'Three tricks of consciousness', *Journal of Consciousness Studies*, **9**, 65–88.
Libet, B., Freeman, A. & Sutherland, K. (ed. 1999), *The Volitional Brain* (Exeter: Imprint Academic).
Maxwell, N. (2001), *The Human World in the Physical Universe: Consciousness, Free Will, and Evolution* (Landham, MD: Rowman and Littlefield).

Editorial Advisory Board:

Bernard J. Baars
Neurosciences Inst. (Cognitive Science)

David Chalmers
Australian National University (Phil.)

Ewert Cousins
Fordham University (Religion)

Daniel C. Dennett
Tufts University (Cognitive Studies)

Margaret Donaldson
Edinburgh University (Psychology)

Peter Fenwick
Maudsley Hospital (Neuropsychology)

Brian Goodwin
Schumacher College (Biology)

Stuart Hameroff
University of Arizona (Anesthesiology)

Erich Harth
Syracuse University (Physics)

Jeremy Hayward
Naropa Institute

Basil Hiley
Birkbeck College (Physics)

Nicholas Humphrey
London School of Economics (Psych)

Piet Hut (Astrophysics)
Institute for Advanced Studies

Robert Kentridge
University of Durham (Psychology)

Christof Koch
CalTech (Neurobiology)

George Lakoff
UC, Berkeley (Linguistics)

Benjamin Libet
UC, San Francisco (Physiology)

Philip Merikle
University of Waterloo (Psychology)

Mary Midgley
University of Newcastle (Philosophy)

Raimon Panikkar
UC, Santa Barbara (Religion)

Roger Penrose
Oxford University (Mathematics)

Geraint Rees, Institute of Cognitive Neuroscience (Neuroscience)

Eleanor Rosch
UC, Berkeley (Psychology)

David Rosenthal, CUNY (Philosophy)

John Searle
UC, Berkeley (Philosophy)

Huston Smith
Syracuse University (Philosophy)

Susan Leigh Star
UC, San Diego (Communications)

Roger Walsh
UC, Irvine (Psychiatry)

Arthur Zajonc
Amherst College (Physics)

Executive Editors

Joseph A. Goguen (Editor in Chief). Department of Computer Science University of California at San Diego, La Jolla, CA 92093-0114, USA. Phone: (858) 534-4197. Fax: (858) 534-7029. Email: goguen@cs.ucsd.edu

Robert K.C. Forman, Director, The Forge Institute, 383 Broadway, Hastings on Hudson, NY 10706, USA. Tel/Fax: (914) 478 7802. Email: Forman@TheForge.org

Keith Sutherland (Publisher). Imprint Academic, PO Box 200, Exeter EX5 5YX, UK. Tel: +44 1392 841600 Email: keith@imprint.co.uk

Managing Editor (address for manuscript submissions and books for review)
Anthony Freeman, Imprint Academic, PO Box 200, Exeter EX5 5YX, UK. Tel: +44 1392 841600. Email: anthony@imprint.co.uk

Associate Editors

Jean *Burns*, 1525 – 153rd Avenue, San Leandro, CA 94578, USA. Tel: (510) 481 7507. Email: jeanbur@earthlink.net

Ivo Mosley (Poetry), Imprint Academic, PO Box 200, Exeter EX5 5YX, UK. Tel: +44 1392 841600. Email: ivomosley@aol.com

Chris Nunn (Book Reviews), Imprint Academic, PO Box 200,Exeter EX5 5YX, UK. Tel: +44 1392 841600. Email: chrisnunn@compuserve.com

Jonathan Shear, Department of Philosophy, Virginia Commonwealth University, Richmond, VA 23284-2025, USA. Tel/Fax: (804) 282 2119. Email: jcs@infionline.net

Annual Subscription Rates (for 12 monthly issues)
Individuals: $99/£62
Institutions: $296/£185
Includes accelerated delivery (UK & USA), surface mail rest of world.
Orders to : Imprint Academic, PO Box 200, Exeter EX5 5YX, UK.
Tel: +44 1392 841600; Fax: 841478; Email: sandra@imprint.co.uk.
Cheques (£ or $US 'Imprint Academic'); VISA/AMEX/MASTERCARD

STYLE SHEET AND GUIDE TO AUTHORS

JCS is aimed at an educated multi-disciplinary readership. Authors should not assume prior knowledge in a subject speciality and should provide background information for their research. The use of technical terms should be avoided or made explicit. Where technical details are essential (for example in laboratory experiments), include them in footnotes or appendices, leaving the text accessible to the non-specialist reader. The same principle should also apply to non-essential mathematics.

Articles should not normally exceed 9,000 words (including footnotes). A short 150 word summary should accompany each submission. In general authors should adhere to the usages and conventions in Fowler's *Modern English Usage* which should be consulted for all questions not covered in these notes.

Footnote numbering should be consecutive superscript throughout the article. References to books and articles should be by way of author (date) or (author, date). Multiple publications from the same year should be labelled (Skinner, 1966a, b, c . . .). A single bibliography at the end should be compiled alphabetically observing the following conventions:

1 References to complete books should take the following form:
  Dennett, D.C. (1998), *Brainchildren* (Cambridge, MA: MIT Press).

2 References to chapters in books should take the following form:
  Wilkes, K. (1995), 'Losing consciousness', in *Conscious Experience*, ed. T. Metzinger (Paderborn: Schöningh).

3 References to articles should take the following form:
  Humphrey, N. (2000), 'How to solve the mind–body problem', *Journal of Consciousness Studies*, **7** (4), pp. 5–20.

SUBMISSION OF MANUSCRIPTS BY EMAIL

Authors are encouraged to email their wordprocessor files (retaining italics, accents, superscripts, footnotes etc.) or PDF files. We cannot currently review LaTex files. Send all submissions to **anthony@imprint.co.uk**.

Where it is necessary to send contributions by normal mail, they should be clearly typed in double spacing. One hard copy should be submitted, plus a copy of the article on disk. This will enable us to email it to editors and reviewers and speed up the review process. Please state what machine and wordprocessing program was used to prepare the text.